How to get
WINNERS, not WHINERS

SHAPING A LEADING AND WINNING CULTURE

A non-conformist collection of insights into how to build leadership and create a winning company culture.

← COMPLICATED

SIMPLE →

"Complexity is the enemy of execution"

Colophon
Design and layout: Buro Jung
Editor: René de Boer & Jac de Ruiter
Publisher: BigBusinessPublishers, Utrecht, The Netherlands
ISBN: 9789493171343

First edition: January 2022
Reprint: January 2024

© Erik Hiep / BigBusinessPublishers

ALL RIGHTS RESERVED
Except as provided for in the Copyright Act
of 1912, no parts of this publication may copied,
stored in an automated database
or be made public, either electronically,
mechanically, through photocopies,
recordings, or any other means, without
prior written permission from the publisher.

INTRODUCTION

Keep it simple

Attempts to change organizations fail in 70% to 80% of all cases. However, the success rate skyrockets when organizations implement change through an integrated approach, where changes in structure, strategy, processes, systems, attitudes and behaviour are more or less simultaneously implemented (Pettigrew, 2001)[1].

Over time as a consultant, I have learned which approaches work and which don't. My main conclusion is that whatever method or model you decide on, it needs to be simple and easy to use. Not only is the emphasis that most change managers place on analysis, strategy, processes and structure overrated, but they often use (or are advised to use) methods that are far too complex to be digested and cascaded down the organization. This harbours the risk of making life for the CEO and the executive team more complicated, not easier.

In this book, I would like to share some plain and simple insights into how to create a winning culture. You'll find practical and easily digestible bits of theory combined with the personal stories of executives from all around the world. They share their leadership experience and how they believe they should guide their teams and manage their organizations. I joined them on their journey. We carved out time to huddle up, discuss scenarios and take action. In this book, I share some of their stories as inspiration for others to succeed as well.

Have a look, read a couple of pages, study some sections, observe, diagnose and get inspired. I hope this book helps when you want to shape a leading and winning culture in your organization, dealing with challenges in your team or trying to find a new way forward for yourself.

Erik Hiep Noordwijk, January 2022

TEAM, TIME AND TEMPERAMENT P.24
David Cameron *Former prime minister of the UK*

IT IS ALWAYS SHOWTIME P.58
Mark Fleiner *CEO of Malvern Panalytical in the USA*

TRUST IS CRUCIAL IN ANY CIRCUMSTANCE P.86
Valeria Flen Silva *CEO of Gloria in Peru*

TALK WITH LEARN FROM THE BEST

When doing my research for this book, I interviewed inspiring leaders from all around the globe about their vision, strategy and experience with change. I have worked with nearly all of them over the past years and was impressed by how they were able to lead and win in the dynamic, international business arena.

The objective of this book is to share with you how these individuals, in a very authentic way, used their personal leadership to create an engaging climate geared to winning. All of them stressed the importance of having a healthy, inspiring and energetic company culture. What do they see as crucial, and how do they generate success?

TO FORGIVE AND BE FORGIVEN P.10
Ingvild Sæther *CEO of Altera Infrastructure in Norway*

CHANGING MAKES US HAPPY P.110
Martin Boehm *Former Dean IE Business School and Rector EBS University*

FAILURE IS NOT AN OPTION P.14
Lex Hoefsloot *CEO Lightyear in the Netherlands*

LEAD MANAGEMENT, DON'T MANAGE LEADERS P.44
Olav Cuiper *Executive Vice President, Chief Client Officer in the Netherlands*

LEAVING NO MAN BEHIND P.96
Jordy Kool *Entrepreneur & Investor in the Netherlands*

WHEN THE GOING GETS TOUGH P.38
Sumeet Mathur *MD FrieslandCampina Middle East in the UAE*

LEADING BY CREATING VALUE P.66
Theo Spierings *Former CEO of Fonterra in New Zealand*

INDEX

INTRODUCTION	5
LEARN FROM THE BEST	6

TO FORGIVE & BE FORGIVEN Ingvild Sæther	10
FAILURE IS NOT AN OPTION Lex Hoefsloot	14
CONTEXT OF ORGANIZATIONS	20
TEAM, TIME & TEMPERAMENT David Cameron	24
COMING UP WITH A GOOD AND SIMPLE PLAN	31
THE RATIONAL AGENDA	34
WHEN THE GOING GETS TOUGH Sumeet Mathur	38
LEAD MANAGEMENT, DON'T MANAGE LEADERS Olav Cuiper	44
THE EMOTIONAL AGENDA	50
10 FATAL LEADERSHIPS FLAWS	56

IT IS ALWAYS SHOWTIME Mark Fleiner	58
LEADING BY CREATING VALUE Theo Spierings	66
THE BEHAVIOURAL AGENDA	70
THE FRAMEWORK FOR WINNING	82
SEVEN CULTURE KILLERS	84
TRUST IS CRUCIAL IN ANY CIRCUMSTANCE Valeria Flen Silva	86
IN THE VUCA WORLD	90
LEAVING NO MAN BEHIND Jordy Kool	96
BITS & BYTES ON PERSONAL LEADERSHIP	102
CHANGING MAKES US HAPPY Martin Boehm	110

EPILOGUE	115
BACKGROUND AND CREDENTIALS	117
INDEX OF LITERATURE	118

TO FORGIVE AND BE FORGIVEN

The double meaning of creating a sustainable environment

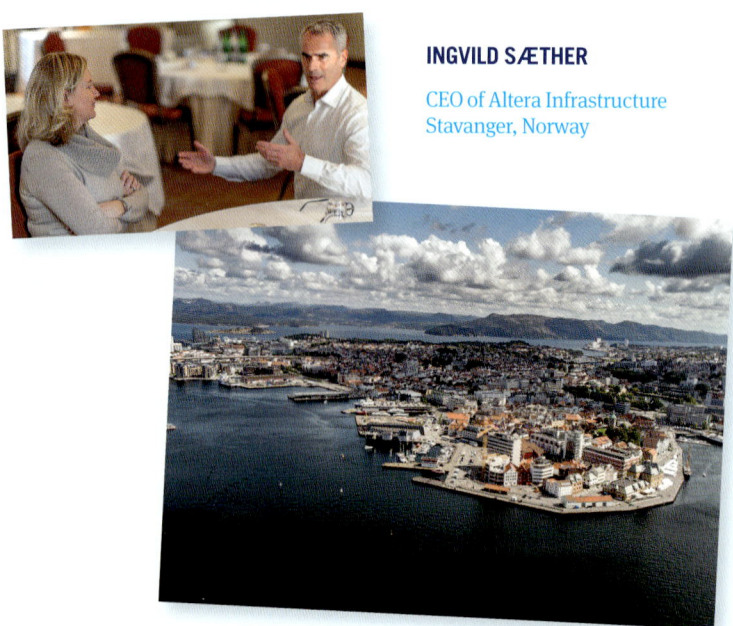

TALK WITH

INGVILD SÆTHER

CEO of Altera Infrastructure
Stavanger, Norway

Since 2017, Ingvild Sæther has been the president and CEO of Altera Infrastructure Group, formerly known as Teekay Offshore Group. The company provides critical infrastructure assets, like tankers, production and storage units, long-distance towing and offshore installation vessels. With Altera, Sæther wants to lead the industry to a sustainable future. Besides caring for earth's environment, she's also been creating a working environment where it's okay to disagree and people feel encouraged to speak their mind.

It was the accumulation of 25 years of experience in the shipping and offshore sector with positions on numerous industry boards and associations that took Ingvild Sæther to the top of Altera Infrastructure in February 2017. It was her first time as a CEO, and she says it can be lonely at the top. 'The first two years were very difficult. The transition from Teekay to Altera was not easy: it wasn't the start-up of a small company – it was actually the transformation of a big global company. But we still had to build everything, from scratch; strategy to the team, from values to culture and from purpose to direction.' Sæther says there were times when she questioned whether she'd be able to push on and whether she was the right person for the job. 'First of all, I kept myself going in the knowledge that I could quit any day. I knew I had a choice. And it was my own. Nobody was forcing me to do something that I didn't like or didn't want, and that was the mindset that kept me going.

The other part was the realisation that there's no perfect CEO. No one has it all, and that thought is quite comforting.' Things started to fall into place after a while, Sæther continues. 'It was like getting my head above the water, starting to understand the connections and the language. It boiled down to the obvious question: what is this about? The answer is that it's all about common sense. So I knew I'd be able to get my head around it.' Looking back at the strenuous first two years, she feels lucky. 'It was a once-in-a-lifetime experience: being able to start a new global company and, at the same time, having the building blocks of a leader in the industry. Wow!'

Sustainable leadership
Altera is on a mission to transform the offshore industry, an area where there is quite some talk about sustainability but not a lot of walk. Sæther acknowledges this but states: 'We put a lot of energy into sustainable leadership. And this is profitable. We've had a lot of good discussions with the Norwegian government, received subsidies and delivered on our promises by designing and building these lower-emission vessels that are powered by LNG and fitted with batteries. So, we do the talk and we do the walk. That makes our people proud of their employer, and it will also bring us new opportunities, maybe even by expanding into new segments.'

Sustainable environment
Besides a sustainable natural environment, Sæther is also dedicated to creating a sustainable working environment. This begins by activating the dialogue within the company, from the top down. 'We have 30 people who can reach out to really everyone in the company. So, it's vital that this group understand where we are going and why, and what we need to do. Furthermore, it's crucial for me to be totally transparent with these people and not try to hide things or smooth them over. They, in turn, need to be able to handle reality and make sure they get their messages straight within the groups they are leading.'

It's about forgiveness

'I talk and think a lot about leadership, but I don't always act the best I could or should. It's hard to live up to your own expectations, especially in stressful situations or when someone is pushing the wrong button.
For example, I can get very engaged in discussions – even forceful and confrontational. The best thing that can happen then is for people to push back. Then I can be myself and get all the perspectives out on the table. When people don't want to confront me, I need to restrain myself, and that takes a lot more energy.'

Searching for solutions and the right path is benefited by constructive conversation where all opinions, insights and perspectives are welcome, says Sæther. 'That means making sure people aren't afraid to speak up and showing a certain amount of forgiveness at the same time. Let me explain: my purpose as a leader is to be there for the team. I do my best, and I want them to do their best. But we're only human. We cannot always be the best version of ourselves; there must be room for experimentation and failure. And there is nothing I love more than to be proven wrong by someone on the team! That's what it's about to me: creating that atmosphere where we feel we can be ourselves.'

FAILURE IS NOT AN OPTION

"Creating a winning team"

TALK WITH

LEX HOEFSLOOT

CEO of Lightyear
Helmond, the Netherlands

The automotive industry is characterised by large players with big budgets for innovation, production and marketing. The entry threshold is high. Nevertheless, breaking that barrier and producing the world's first long-range solar car is exactly what Dutch automaker Lightyear wanted to do.

Two years of hard work, determination and persistence culminated in the summer of 2019 in the unveiling of the prototype of the world's first long-range solar car. 'Our car, the Lightyear One, is completely different', says Lightyear CEO Lex Hoefsloot. Indeed, each wheel has its own electric motor. The car is relatively low and therefore more aerodynamic. The roof is covered with solar cells, but the car can also be charged via an external power source, like other electric cars.

Pioneering

In 2016, Lex Hoefsloot had just taken up his idea for building a new car on solar energy. He started off with a small team of five founders, which they pioneered into a company that now has over 150 employees. The founders knew each other from Eindhoven University of Technology, where they designed a car for a solar race in Australia. The aim of that race was to travel as far as possible with a solar-powered car. The students thought that the same technology would also be feasible for passenger vehicles. And so it happened. The starting point was the same: drive as many kilometres as possible on solar power. Lightyear views itself as a group of engineers who saw a way to combat climate change. The team saw something that could be done, and they're doing it.

Mission first
The Lightyear team's focus on the mission and will to win are probably among their most important characteristics. Hoefsloot: 'We're a tech company on a mission: to create clean transportation for everyone. And this is super important. We need to figure out how Lightyear can expand while still maintaining our focus on winning and on our mission.'

Hoefsloot's determination is special. To him, failure is simply not an option. Similar mindsets are among those who explore space, as well as in the military.

Winning team
In regard to creating a winning team, Hoefsloot confesses that there was a lack of diversity at first. The initial team consisted entirely of Dutch millennials, mostly former technical university students, all capable and willing to work 24/7. They had a similar tech mindset, a certain dry sense of humour and a huge drive. On top of that, they shared a common belief system about why to fight climate change and how to capitalise on technology. This uniformity proved very powerful during the start-up phase. It was easy to align the team, and everyone was quick on their feet. The rules of how to behave and what was expected were unwritten yet very clear. Then, during the scale-up phase, the team needed to expand in size,

skills and quality, so more diversity was needed in the initial team, as well as in the rest of the company.

Growth Officer Maijke Receveur is responsible for getting Lightyear's workforce up and running. She's been working relentlessly to set the company up for victory in this next stage of its development. The key question here is how to create an environment where everyone feels at home, where equality rules and where team members can play on their strengths most of the time. 'The company values are our guiding principles not only when hiring people but also when designing our workforce structure', she notes.

About high trust
When you create a high-trust environment in your organization, everything moves at a faster pace. This is helpful if you live in a red ocean where time is scarce. High-trust environments also foster honesty, playfulness and spontaneity: essential ingredients if you need innovation on a daily basis. If you're on a super-important mission and you need to pioneer creative solutions with your team, this high-trust environment is a must. Everyone in the company needs to have that same spirit to make it happen.

It's one thing to create such an environment, but quite another to maintain it and continue developing and growing it in a crowded, high-pressure marketplace. Lightyear is doing all this and more – as we speak. The 'Lightyear spirit' is about a team of ambitious pioneers working on an important mission and knowing they will achieve it. This spirit is the driving factor behind their success.

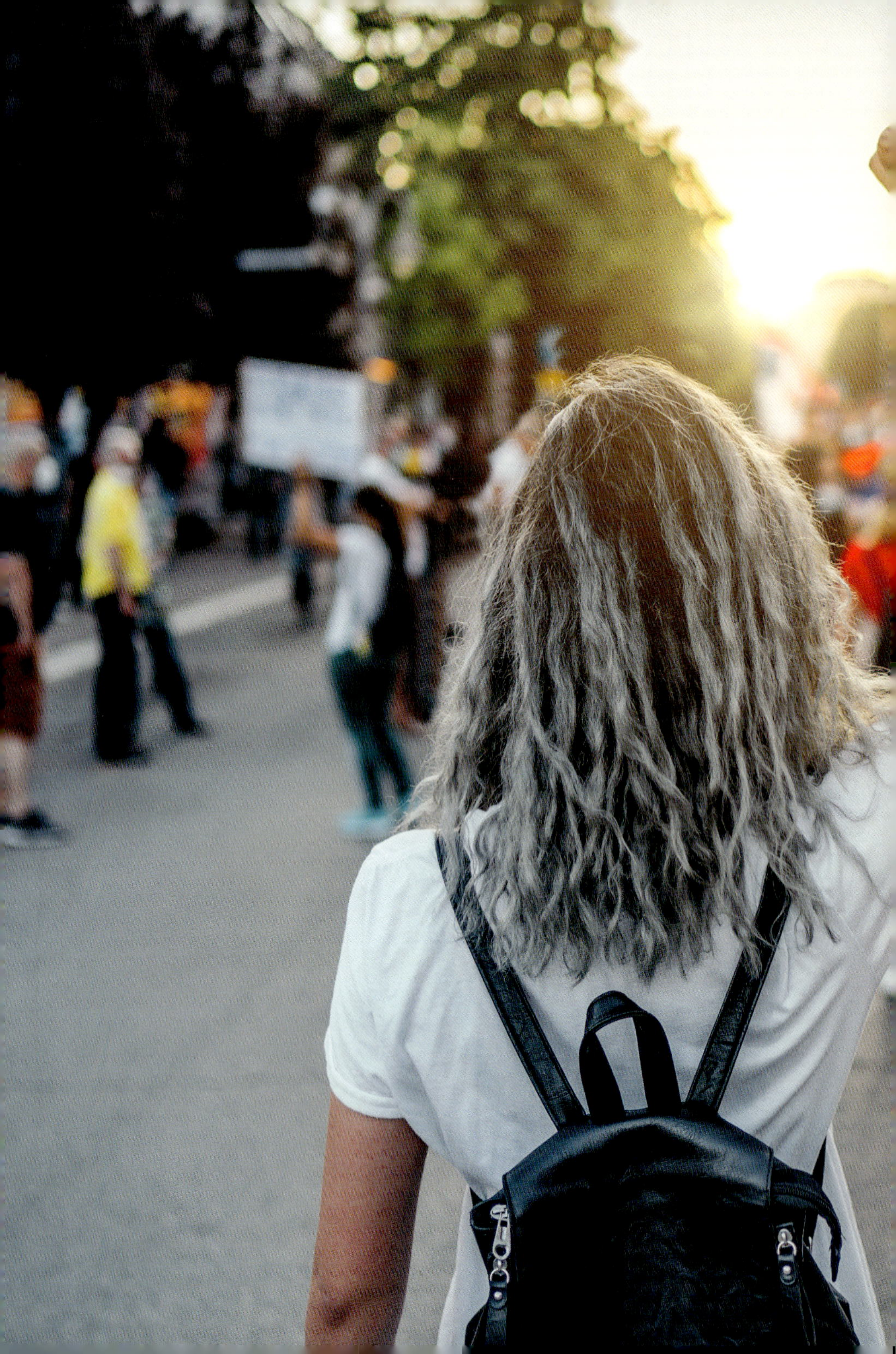

"This is not an era of change, it's a change of era"

CONTEXT OF ORGANIZATIONS

The VUCA world

In general, all organizations have internal and external problems to deal with. The big external challenge for all companies around the globe is that we are living in extraordinary times and in a VUCA world.

VUCA:
Volatile: the nature, speed, volume, magnitude and dynamics of change
Uncertain: issues and events are difficult to predict
Complex: organizations are surrounded by chaos and confounded issues
Ambiguous: the haziness of reality and the mixed meanings of conditions

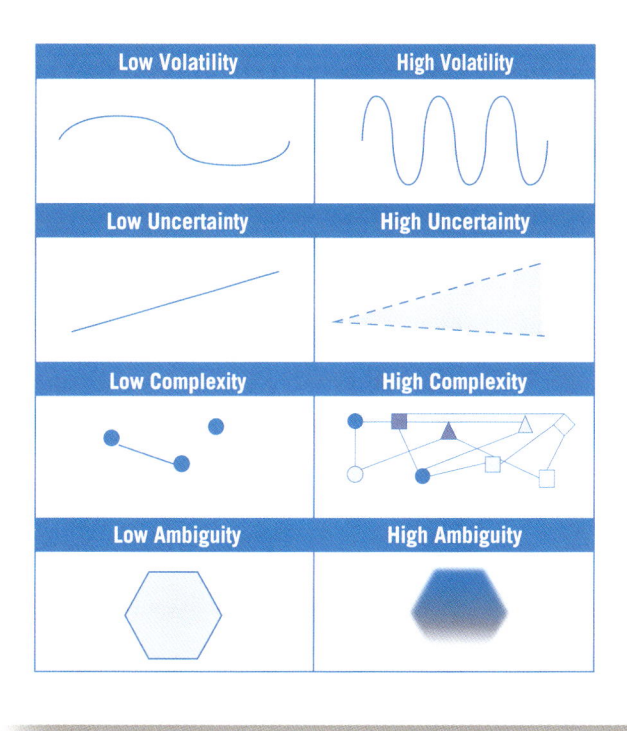

Low Volatility	High Volatility
Low Uncertainty	High Uncertainty
Low Complexity	High Complexity
Low Ambiguity	High Ambiguity

Understanding the nature of the problems you are facing, is the first step in overcoming them. It helps when you need to deal with challenges in the marketplace to analyze and frame them. This way you understand the bigger picture faster and your response is probably more effective.
What kind of problem do we detect?

The 'fire in the house' problem
This is a clear, visible and urgent problem – in a way, the kind of problem that we love. It's clear what we have at hand and what needs to be done. Action to put out the fire does not require lengthy analysis, and by fighting shoulder to shoulder and working hard, we can put the fire out. Then we can look back and feel proud of ourselves, our team and the organization for successfully solving this problem.

The 'Rubik's Cube' problem
The Rubik's Cube problem presents a somewhat different situation.
The problem requires thorough analysis to solve. Assessments,
SWOT analyses and deep dives are needed to map this kind of problem.

You'll probably also need to design an intelligent roadmap with milestones in the process. This calls for taskforces with project plans as well as pilots and co-pilots to lead these teams and manage alignment. If we keep on going, work through setbacks and keep the budget under tight control, we might be able to overcome this problem.

The 'wicked' problem
The hardest is what we can call the 'wicked' problem. A wicked problem is one that does not seem to have a solution. Examples of this kind of problem are how to prevent a terrorist attack or deal with a new virus that suddenly appears and spreads.

Where to start and how to wrap your head around this one? How confident can you be when designing a solution – one that really needs to work? Here you might have to invite outsiders in to better understand the problem and then design multiple scenarios: trial and error seems the only viable way out. And you may never really be sure whether you can solve the problem. On the flip side, hope is not a strategy, so you'll need to switch into action mode no matter what.

Internal challenges

As if that wasn't enough, there are also internal problems that companies need to tackle. Three internal problems that almost always exist:

1. **The team is not a team:** there is no trust among colleagues, among teams or with leadership.
2. **The strategy is not clear:** there is no direction that people can embrace and take action on.
3. **The communication is deficient:** there is no understanding, especially of what is expected.

How to…

The only good solution for dealing with all of this is to come up with a good and simple plan. But that's easier said than done. Have a look at page 31 for some possible next steps.

TEAM, TIME AND TEMPERAMENT

TALK WITH

DAVID CAMERON

former prime minister of the UK

In 2018 I had the pleasure of interviewing David Cameron, the former British prime minister, live in front of a 2000+ audience. I have taken the liberty of sharing the essence of Cameron's view on leadership while adding some of my own insights.

In light of the changes currently taking place in economic and business models, leadership has become a hot topic of late. Leaders certainly need tech skills to face the challenge of digitalisation, but they must also be equipped to handle decision-making, which remains a crucial issue in every organization. What are the essential skills of leadership? This eternal question remains as relevant as ever in the business world. In fact, business leadership has much in common with leadership in the political arena and even in the personal sphere.

Every day, we all find ourselves having to make decisions of varying degrees of importance. In the political world, these decisions tend to be somewhat more profound, since they involve a wide range of people and have an impact on their quality of life. Nevertheless, the fundamental skills set of leadership applies across the board – in business, in politics and in personal matters.

So, what are the skills that make up this holy grail? David Cameron explained that every leader has a unique personality, which comprises a multitude of variables and traits that influence his or her management style. He cited three immutable principles associated with betterdecision-making: team, time and temperament.

The team over the individual
To ensure the best possible conditions, the team must always take precedence over the individual. The ego must be considered from the perspective of the group. Leaders should be considered incredible, not on their own merit but as a result of the people that surround them.

The configuration of work teams is therefore an essential ingredient for success. This is a key task in companies, in politics, in personal affairs and even in sports. In Cameron's words, 'Create a team that would do anything for you by doing the same for them.' And this includes people not necessarily aligned with the leader.

It's important not to ignore anyone. When making difficult decisions, don't shy away from the extremes. It's better to build bridges and work to overcome possible divisions. It's more practical to find solutions to complaints than to the underlying questions. Swallow your pride and don't worry about your next appointment or re-election. Never silence your antagonists, and be prepared to negotiate with them when necessary. Only with this approach will you be able to create a diverse, reliable team capable of facing conflicts effectively.

Time and lack thereof
Building a perfectly cohesive team takes time, the second major theme of Cameron's reflections. This may seem obvious, but time is a highly significant factor in planning a project. Investing time when necessary can lead to a better approach. There are so many variables, option and lines of action, which the team must revise a thousand times. Experience shows that improvisation is not the way to exercise effective leadership.

This is why most organizations develop plans for the long term. Returning to the subject of politics, Cameron recalled that Winston Churchill spent five long days in 1940 debating with his team about how to combat Hitler during the Second World War. 'The most difficult decision I had to make was sending troops into battle', Cameron noted. Outside the context of armed conflicts, important decisions now tend to be made in just ten minutes. The rapid pace of modern decision-making is, in part, a consequence of the lack of time cited by many leaders.

Although it may be tedious, when making decisions it is essential to take your time and think. Fight back against the stress and examine the potential consequences of your choice.

The mirror effect

Finally, the former prime minister touched on his third key theme: temperament. The ability to withstand pressure during conflicts and important processes is a fundamental part of being a leader. Mastery of a situation involves, among other things, remaining calm so that you can deal with it. Bosses are like mirrors held up to their teams: if they fall victim to panic, the people around them may follow suit, setting in motion an undesirable dynamic.

Don't surrender to the crisis; work hard and convey serenity to the people around you. Focus on what you really have to do, and dedicate all your energy to it. This will give you strength and supply your team with greater mental capacity. In the face of adversity, work on your soft skills – humour, fun, creativity, etc. – to generate a better climate and become more relatable. Soft skills are more important than ever, as they enable you to adapt to the pace of change.

> These tips cannot ensure success – this is not an exact science – but they can guarantee a culture and a leadership style that are highly valued in today's world, for bosses, political authorities, parents and for human beings in general.

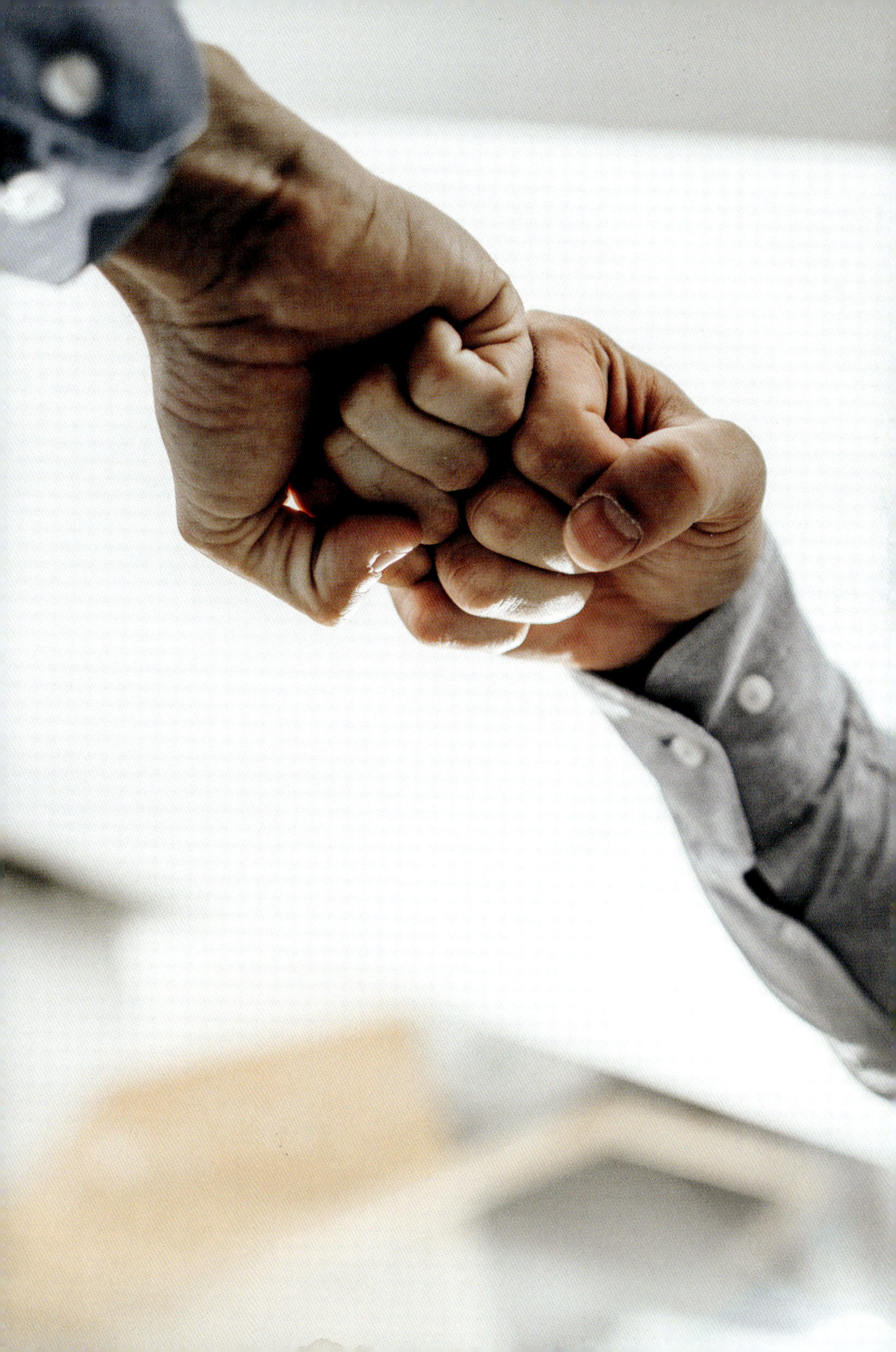

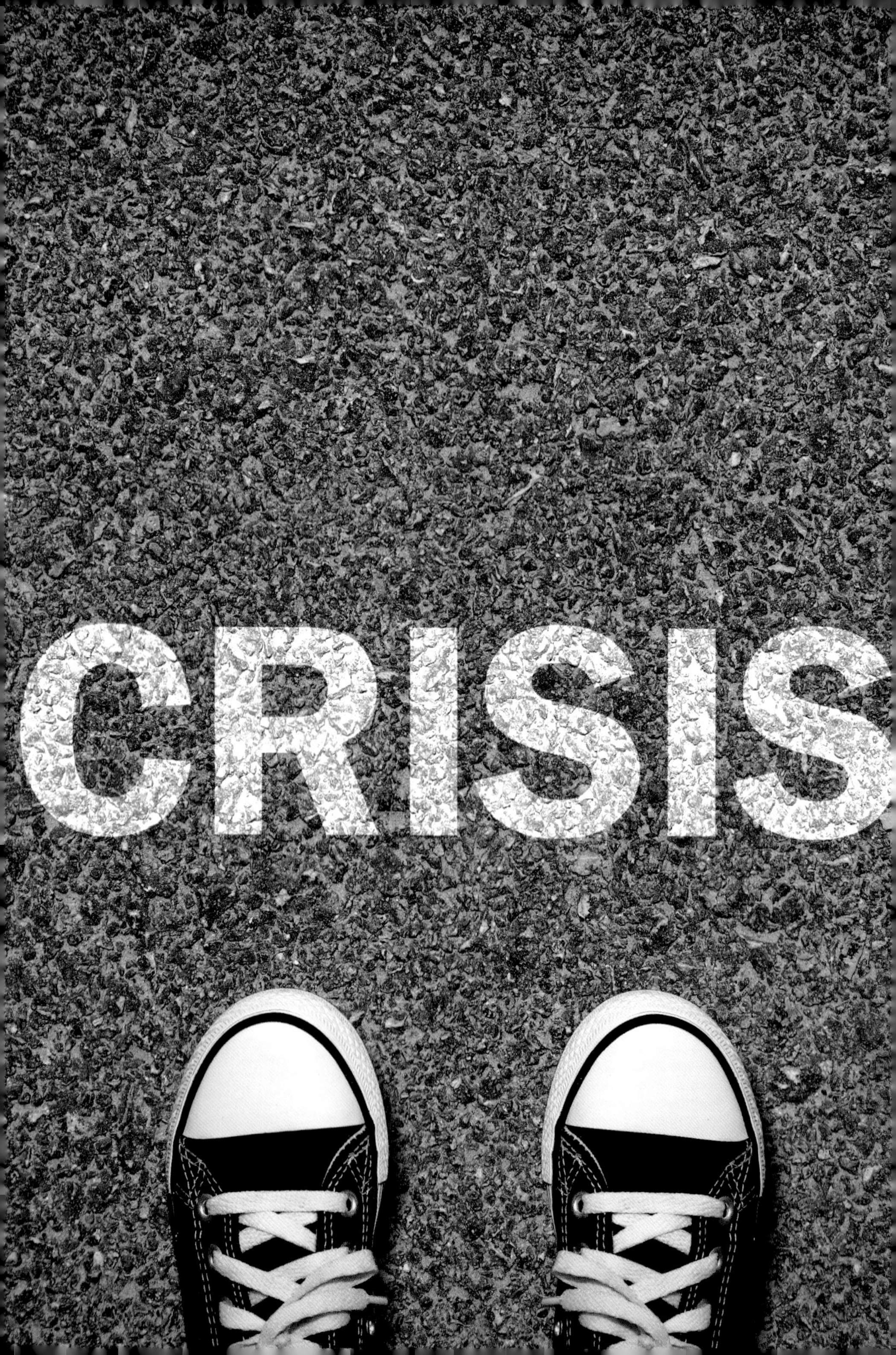
CRISIS

COMING UP WITH A GOOD AND SIMPLE PLAN

Way back in the 20th century, I attended the Royal Military Academy in the Netherlands to become an infantry officer. First of all, we were taught that brawn, bravery and perseverance are all essential on the battlefield but that the key differentiator is adaptability. Furthermore, to create a winning strategy, it's paramount to hammer out a very clear and simple plan.

Here are some interesting parallels to the things I learned when I started my career as a management consultant. In our volatile world, the ability to adapt to a shifting business landscape is vital. So is the ability to keep things simple. The world around us is usually fuzzy, foggy and complicated. It's easy to lose sight of the bigger picture. When a crisis hits, this leads to stress, pressure and the need to manage many contingencies all at once – with the risk of losing control. In such situations, it's best to fall back on one basic rule: simple stuff works.

Making a good and simple plan is never easy though. It takes a lot to come up with a solid plan with full clarity and a straight direction. What can we do to create clarity? Let's start by looking at the various agendas.

Keep calm, never hurry

As a leader, you must avoid panic and stress. Of course you have to be able to enter the pressure cooker and quickly discuss various scenarios with capable, passionate professionals. But when you emerge from it, you must again be calm, composed and in control; fast-paced but never in a hurry.

The three agendas

Crucial to the success of change is having three calendars in conjunction (Aristotle, Ars Rhetorica Oxford, March 1963)[2]:

1.   **The rational agenda**
2.   **The emotional agenda**
3.   **The behavioural agenda**

The rational agenda represents 'the case for change'. Why is change necessary? Where is the pain? Or where are the opportunities? What should we change? It brings us to classic organizational issues such as mission, vision, strategy, structure, system, operations, markets and customers.

Why are we here, how do we play and what are we going to do? Generating success is about clarity on Simon Sinek's why, how and what. These three components need to be clear and consistent:

Why are we here?
Our purpose is key, engaging and important.

How do we play the game?
Our leadership manifesto is about how we lead and work together.

What are we going to do?
We will engage and involve everyone with our simple and effective plan.

The emotional agenda covers the heads and hearts of individual people, from top to bottom. This agenda should be given even more importance than the first. In practice, however, it's usually the other way around. To create a winning company, a winning culture or change successfully, you and all your staff need to be 100% committed. Why you do what you do, what you all stand for, what you are trying to achieve and how to make this all work: this needs to cascade down to every single person in the company.

The behavioural agenda is about the actual change of attitude and behaviour we ask of our people and of ourselves, as their leaders. It's about the company culture and the mechanisms that align people to accomplish the organization's purpose. It's about aspiration, values, qualities, development, delegation and communication. All aspects of group processes, like roles, rules, rewards and recognition, are part of this agenda.

Let's start by diving into the rational agenda: the case for change.

THE CASE FOR CHANGE

THE
RATIONAL
AGENDA

Back to basics

If everything around you diverts into complexity, go back to basics.

Stress is the natural human response to a fuzzy, foggy and complicated world. Unfortunately, it can make us lose control and lose sight of the bigger picture. In these difficult and unprecedented times, it's easy to lose track of things and become overwhelmed by incidents and contingencies that need to be managed.

So, what are we focusing on? Will we subconsciously allow fear and anxiety to grab our attention? Or will we make conscious decisions about what we really need and then dedicate our time, energy and effort to this new way forward? Of course, the latter is what leaders need to do. Leaders and followers want speed, clarity and direction. But first we must take our time, brainstorm and think things over. Carve out time to really think things through.

It takes a lot to come up with a solid plan with full clarity and a straight direction. I use a tried and tested military framework. Whenever a military unit prepares for a mission, they draft their plan and focus on five things to create a clear direction: situation; mission; execution; administration and logistics; and command and communication. (www.ie.edu/building-resilience/knowledge)[3]

In the past thirty years, I've learned that this works equally well in business. I've used it whenever I needed to come up with a business solution, a new action plan or a new way forward for a company. It's easy to use and creates clarity and direction for everyone involved. Here's how it works:

1. Situation: overview & context
Describe the current situation with respect to your market, the competition, technology, business development, marketing, HR and your P&L. Come up with a situation report with a clear and solid overview and a relevant context that makes sense for your business.

2. Mission: assignment & objective
Define what your mission is about and what exactly you are setting out to accomplish. What are the key objectives and intended effects? This needs to be super clear and inspiring!

3. Execution: plan & how to win
This is the part where you develop your game plan for accomplishing the mission, having considered the current situation. First, develop a start-to-finish scheme for tackling the problem that you need to overcome in pursuit of your mission. Once the plan is prepared, assign broad tasks. If you have key personnel, assign these broad tasks to them and allow them to come up with their own individual plans.

4. Administration and logistics: resources & requirements
Review the execution plan. What resources, means and requirements do you need to execute your plan successfully? In the military this is about the 4 b's: beans, bullets, band-aids and bad guys (i.e. what to do with them once you capture them).

5. Command & communication:
leadership & providing clarity on the way forward

Identify for your team, staff and employees who the leader is, including what and when things need to be communicated and to whom.

> This framework (based on extensive experience) will help you to avoid complexity, get back to basics and win in the marketplace. And... keep this in mind: no plan survives first contact with the enemy. In other words: don't fall in love with your plan. Always be prepared to adapt and adjust on the fly.

WHEN THE GOING GETS TOUGH...

"About staying relevant"

TALK WITH

SUMEET MATHUR

Managing Director
FrieslandCampina Middle East
Dubai, United Arab Emirates

In everyday life, you see who your friends are when you need them most. In business life, you see who the true leaders are when a real, severe and unexpected problem occurs. Think of any setback – a disastrous pandemic, for instance – and there will be leaders who duck while others step up. Part of the latter category, Sumeet Mathur leads by example. But that does not mean placing himself in front of the troops. 'For the most part, it's all about communication, connecting and informing people and letting them do what they know best.'

Born and raised in a middle-class family in Delhi, India, Mathur learnt early on that hard work and diligence will be your only partners. Like most other youngsters, he was indoctrinated with the idea that there was no fallback. 'Coming from a resource-constrained background, my mind was set that the only way to succeed is through hard work: giving it your best. My key mission during my youth was to get the best possible education and a successful career.' Another aspect of his upbringing was to value people as equals – not for what they possess. This basic human value of respect was to stay with Mathur throughout his life.

Humane approach
Humility is the dominating characteristic in his approach towards others. He is well-known for being an attentive listener to whatever anybody has to say. 'The basic here is that I always try to be respectful. In addition, I always ask a lot of questions, especially to the frontliners, since they know the market the best. I love feedback. As the saying goes, it's the breakfast of champions.'

'I'm certainly not omniscient, nor do I try to be. In fact, quite the contrary is true. Yes, I might spot a good idea or two, but the people who are doing the work tend to know best.

That's why I always want to have people around who are smarter than me; and it's my responsibility to make sure that they are well informed.
They must have every bit of information they need to do the right things, make the right decisions for the company.

Over-communicating
Faced with COVID and measures like working from home, Mathur decided fairly quickly to intensify the communication routine with his management. Their meetings turned from monthly to weekly. The objective was to make sure that everybody knew about everything – good and bad news alike.
'If you want your company to be agile, to act and react to unexpected circumstances and thrive, you have to make sure that people are confident enough. And that starts by keeping them informed about everything that's happening.'

He firmly states that there is no such thing as over-communication, especially about strategic priorities. 'I emphasise again and again what we stand for, where we are going, what our road map and directions are. Repeating my message is key. That's how I make sure everybody understands the context and keeps focused on the right actions.'

Managing cultures, personalities and faces
Mathur and his team coordinate the operation of FrieslandCampina Middle East from the office in Dubai. When asked how skilful a leader must be to manage a workforce of at least 20 nationalities, he seems surprised.
'I don't look at nationality. I look at people, all of whom I treat the same

with basic human respect. People differ far more by personality than by nationality.' For instance, before arriving in Dubai, he was advised that whenever negotiating something in the Middle East you must never make the other person lose face.

'Quite frankly, I have yet to come across a culture where it's acceptable to make someone lose face. By stereotyping people based on their nationalities, we create biases and lose the opportunity to understand them as individuals.'

Managing self and your relevance
Sharing his thoughts on leadership, Mathur divides that into three dimensions. 'There's work – in the sense of enterprise, teams and individuals – and then family and then self. Looking back, the first two or three decades of my career were mostly about work and family.
Sure, I could have spent six hours on the golf course every Sunday relaxing and staying fit, but I chose to spend that time with my children while they were growing up. Now that they're becoming more independent, I try to dedicate more time to my own vitality, such as through sports, from tennis to yoga.'

'In my opinion, taking care of "self" is also about staying relevant. In our business – and in many others – the future is digital and based on data analytics. Forecasting customer needs, for instance, will be crucial, and better tools are rapidly being released. We need to grow as a savvy organization, not only by attracting and hiring talented people but also as individuals. So as a professional, I want to stay up to date. That means investing in and digitally transforming myself.'

"No plan survives first contact with the enemy"

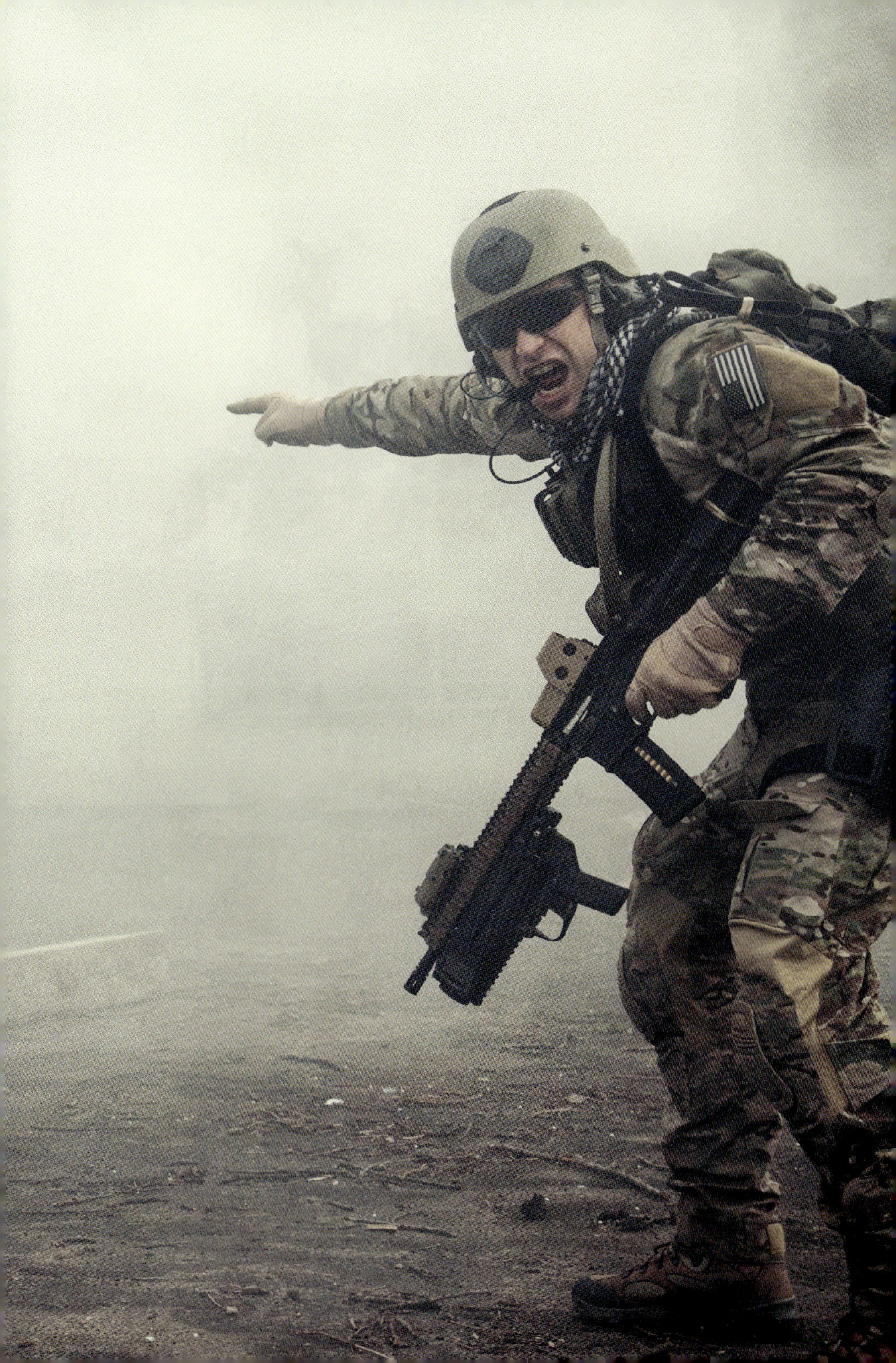

LEAD MANAGEMENT, DON'T MANAGE LEADERS

TALK WITH

OLAV CUIPER

Executive Vice President,
Chief Client Officer
Amsterdam, the Netherlands

We all know, or at least feel that leading and management are being cultivated from different talents. Olav Cuiper is one of those leaders who knows exactly what his limitations are and how to create the circumstances where management can thrive. And can act decisively in today's rapidly changing and highly competitive business environment.

We're all used to hearing how important management and leadership are for guiding teams through volatility. While there's no denying that both competencies are extremely valuable, they're completely different. People who are able to excel at both are a rare breed. So in most circumstances, you should not want a leader to manage or expect a manager to be an inspirational leader.

Because more often than not, great leaders do not have the skills (or ambition to learn how) to manage people and teams. And top managers tend to lack the inspirational qualities, insights and the vision to drive an organization forward. This can be seen not only in start-ups but also in larger companies that need to adapt to their fast-changing environment. In a VUCA world, it is the leaders who create trust, motivation and inspiration with a defined and clear vision, and the managers who are entrusted with the complexity of everyday business and making the smart and sometimes tough decisions. Both leaders and managers are vital to the success of a business. And both roles must be visible and accessible: always in action mode, as they listen to their teams and employees and serve as an example for others throughout the company.

Clarity is crucial
Olav Cuiper, executive vice president and head of EMEA of Reinsurance Group of America (RGA), is one of those leaders who understands that his strength lies in leading – not managing. In a recent conversation, he explained the importance of providing clarity as a leader, particularly in times of volatility.

Just before the COVID pandemic, Cuiper had already started working on his vision for how to move RGA EMEA into the next decade. RGA is a very successful company. But even with one acquisition after the other and steady profits, Cuiper was convinced that things needed to be shaken up: the company needed to evolve faster and change along with the business environment. He sensed the risk of complacency.

With his top management, Cuiper created a new strategic grid, which is a programme of projects around a clear vision for how the organization needed to change to stay relevant in the next five to ten years.
'We knew where to go, and we needed to involve everyone in the company to get there. But two things were going to make that a bit challenging. First, we have a very diverse company with offices in Europe, the Middle East, Asia and South Africa. Communication had to reach out to all of them. Second, there was no real sense of urgency. We were doing well, so why change? Here the pandemic worked in our favour. It paved the way for resetting our mindset, since we all learnt during 2020 that not only is change a constant; it's also accelerating.'

When the pandemic completely changed the working environment, Cuiper had to focus on making sure that every single person in the company understood the purpose and goals and how to get there.

He explained that connecting with people and teams is crucial for leaders. 'It starts with designing a strategy together that provides clarity and direction. Then we really had to connect the global, regional and local teams.

Since I couldn't travel to have my regular talks with management and employees, we had to create a new way of communicating. The first thing I did was to stay as visible and present as I could, both online and through internal media.'

He became more empathetic in his words to employees, as he acknowledged the changes at work and home due to the pandemic. 'Like myself, most of them were working from home, talking to their computer screen all day in confinement. I admit, this was the first time in my career that I advised people to take a break, take a walk in the park, get or stay fit, read a book or start working on mindfulness.'

Decision-making
While he focused on internal communications, Cuiper and his team emphasised speed in decision-making. RGA's business of reinsurance takes place in a time span of years rather than days. The concern was that teams would wait until the pandemic was over to make important changes or decisions, which would set the company back when what it needed was to push forward and develop.

'We made sure that we showed trust. The continuing profits were helpful, but we especially emphasised that we had great confidence in people's capabilities and really made a point of delegating decisions to the teams.' Cuiper's personal strategy is to delegate decision-making whenever possible. 'It's not that I'm insecure or in the habit of dodging my responsibilities. I simply trust the professionals in my teams to make the best decisions. They often have more in-depth information and a hands-on feel for the context.'

This attitude gives leaders like Cuiper more room to focus on the bigger picture. This is particularly important in times of uncertainty when a host of fluctuating variables can cloud judgement. Being able to rely on the right manager to make the right decision is key, of course, and when done well it enables those managers to be the ones to help their teams reach organizational goals while preventing burnout and demotivation.

While intrinsically linked to leadership, management requires a slightly different skills set, including knowing when to multitask, when to delegate and how to prioritise. The pandemic has brought a plethora of new problems for teams, and leaders must quickly identify the issues and then create a strategy for the managers to tackle these issues. When prioritising, a good leader can choose how long is necessary for a well-thought-out decision to be made before falling behind the rest of the world.

The importance of this choice is magnified by what Cuiper calls the big decisions. 'When in a restaurant, do you choose fish or meat for your main course? That's quite an easy decision because there's no real lasting impact. Nevertheless, you see people hesitating about this choice like it's a matter of life and death.

I'm exaggerating a little, but it's to help you understand that once in a while there are decisions that you really need to prepare for. These are the decisions that define success or shape your destiny. Before making these big decisions, make sure you're fit and balanced. And avoid being frustrated or angry – or even worse, being driven by fear. Only in this balanced state will you be able to take the time to gather the information you need and think it over. Don't waste it.'

Leadership is for all
The pandemic has shown that we live in complex times. But the truth of it is that the business world has long been volatile and disruptive. The pandemic has only heightened this uncertainty and made it necessary for individuals to become leaders themselves. Cuiper believes that leadership should be an aspiration for all of us. 'Today we're seeing changes happen in two weeks that would normally take a couple of years or wouldn't happen at all. That means everyone needs to take the lead, no matter what their job.'

WANTED: A BUSINESS AND COMMUNICATION STRATEGY

THE ♡ EMOTIONAL AGENDA

Mindset of leaders

Every leader has an emotional state that is derived from a certain mindset. This mindset consists of a set of beliefs like:

- I'm a leader, regardless of where or when.
- First of all, I know how to lead myself.
- If we lose or fail, it's only preparation for the better.
- As a human being I have this instinct,
  but what is right in this case: fight or flight?
- Mental state determines result. I have to be positive.
- Are we playing not to lose, or to win?

It all starts with great and inspiring leadership that makes people feel strong and self-confident. The role of leadership is to enhance self-esteem and unleash the potential of each individual in the organization: making sure everyone is able to do their best and willing to go the extra mile. It will bring to the company what they can do best. Everyone needs to be able to play to their strengths, often and a lot. That's how you win and achieve strong results from the bottom up.

Leading or influencing people has a lot to do with setting their agenda. Leaders (like news media) generally are in a position to tell people what they should think about. This is not the same as telling them what to think, or to think alike. To get to the next phase of alignment, you have to provide a context for discussion and deliberation, all the while setting the stage for understanding. By providing focus and an environment for reporting and storytelling, you can influence how your audience understands and evaluates it. Leaders influence others and the world around them by telling an effective story, inspiring them with their ideas and putting the agenda into action.

Leaders need to be strategic in their communication style and message. They must not only set an agenda; they must also prime and frame it. They know they need both a business strategy and a strategy for communicating. So, leaders need to know when to push and when to pull, when to talk and when to be quiet and listen.

GOLDEN OLDIE

Although it originates from the early 1970s (yes, developed fifty years ago by Hersey & Blanchard)[4], situational leadership provides an approach, or rather several approaches, for leaders who want to do the right thing at the right time. This simple 4-box leadership setup works like magic if you really use it as intended. Strangely enough, however, a lot of leaders still seem quite reluctant to do that. Their leadership therefore often results in micro-management, mistrust or disconnect. The right application of situational leadership will stretch your people just the way they need to be stretched. This way you can delegate better, further unleash people's potential and create a high-energy climate.

In short, Hersey and Blanchard characterised four types of leadership styles:

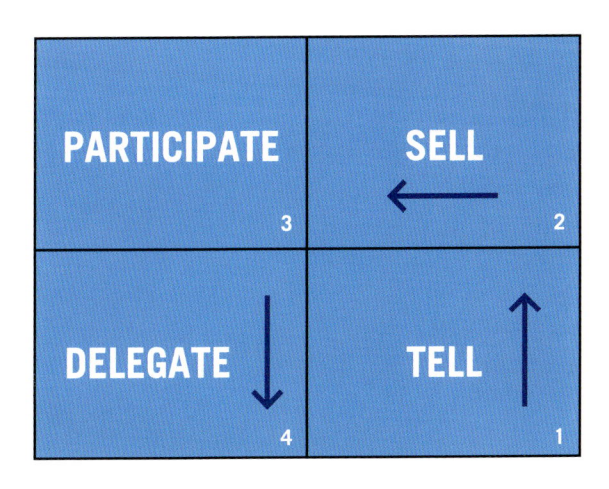

PARTICIPATE 3	SELL ← 2
DELEGATE ↓ 4	TELL ↑ 1

Telling is characterised by one-way communication in which the leader defines the roles of the individual or group and provides the what, how, why, when and where to do the task.

Selling while the leader is still providing the direction, he or she is now using two-way communication and giving the socio-emotional support that will allow the individual or group being influenced to buy into the process.

Participating this is now shared decision-making about how to accomplish the task; the leader provides fewer task behaviours while maintaining high relationship behaviour.

Delegating the leader is still involved in decisions; however, the process and responsibility have been passed to the individual or group. The leader stays involved to monitor progress.

Changing and bonding

Classical change theory often states that people are reluctant to change. This is often not the case. People do not always naturally resist change. Most of them will embrace it if they see and understand the urgency or the benefits of change. It is important to make this clear by being concrete and telling this over and over again.

People also have the urge to belong: they want to join the club or be part of a movement. Thus, they also want to commit to shared goals. To nurture a climate for belonging and committing, the dialogue has to be one of mutual respect, with leadership that shows curiosity and compassion.

LEADERSHIP TRAINING IS A MUST

An organization gets better as each individual member gets better. Developing leaders from within the organization is therefore a priority for driving change. Leadership development should be an integral part of the business strategy. Based on years of experience working with leadership teams, I see five consistent leadership competencies (inspired by Zenger and Folkman's white paper)[5] as critical for driving change and building a winning culture:

ACHIEVER — high-energy and laser-focused

CHANGE AGENT — has an inspiring vision for the way forward

PROFESSIONAL — fully understands the business

COMMUNICATOR — engages, educates and empowers audiences

TEAM PLAYER — trusts others and is trustworthy

Ten fatal Leadership flaws

Leaders with fatal flaws have the lowest employee engagement, customer satisfaction, employee retention and productivity. The bottom line is that the organization pays a high price for keeping them in leadership roles. And from a personal point of view, they'll experience serious limitations on their career progress while getting minimum enjoyment from their work. The 10 fatal leadership flaws[6] most commonly identified by Jack Zenger's research are:

THE 10 FATAL LEADERSHIP FLAWS

1 Not inspiring due to a lack of energy and enthusiasm.

2 Accepting mediocre performance in place of excellent results.

3 Lack of clear vision and direction.

4 Loss of trust stemming from perceived bad judgment and poor decisions.

5 Not a collaborative team player.

6 Not a good role model (failure to walk the talk).

7 No self-development and learning from mistakes.

8 Lacking inter-personal skills.

9 Resistant to new ideas, thus did not lead change or innovate.

10 Focus is on self, not the development of others.

"IT IS ALWAYS SHOWTIME"

"No one has to adapt to me"

TALK WITH

MARK FLEINER

CEO of Malvern Panalytical
Ohio, USA

Imagine you're leading a world-class high-tech company of 3,000 people, most of whom have more expertise than you do regarding the products, services and the needs of highly specialised customers. What could be your biggest contribution? 'My main task is to take the friction out of the work. That means I have to listen, listen and listen again. And I must do that very carefully.'

This story was penned with Mark Fleiner sitting at his computer at home: the same way he spent most of his working hours the past eleven months. In May 2020, Fleiner started as the president of Malvern Panalytical, a world-leading analytical instrumentation and automation solutions provider. Working from home must have been quite a challenge for a business leader who says he's a big fan of 'servant leadership', but he's cheerful and eager to share his way of 'moving people'.

Nevertheless, he confirms that the regular online meetings can be stressful and tiring. 'The other day I was in conference after conference for about five to six hours, without a single pit stop. When I finally got the chance for a break, a message from one of our most valuable talents popped up on my screen. He wanted to talk one-on-one.

As his boss, I could have told him we'd talk later – but that's not my style. I want to be available all the time. And what do you think? This great, highly appreciated co-worker was worried about his performance for the company. What would have happened in his mind if I had postponed our virtual get-together? Or told him to ask my secretary to make an appointment?'

Fleiner says this aspect of his role has become increasingly important. In the two-dimensional space of online meetings there is hardly any room for informal levelling afterwards. 'Most of the time when we leave a virtual meeting, we only have ourselves to talk to. And self-talk can be very harsh: we are our own worst critics.'

Self-talk
Fleiner believes it's crucial for leaders to provide an atmosphere in which people can be confident. 'This responsibility has become even more important since we're all working at home. People have been deprived of the chance to reflect informally with one or two colleagues. After leaving an online meeting we're on our own; we can't walk over to the coffee machine and chat about what had just been said. So then we start this self-talk: "Did I say the right things? I wonder what they thought about my remarks on this and that?"

We all have these two voices in our head: one's your advocate and the other is your critic. It's easy to let the latter dominate and lower your confidence – and your effectiveness. If you're attentive, it's amazing what you can do for people in your company, especially in the current circumstances. So make them feel better, get them flying.'

Adapting abroad
To illustrate his way of being a servant leader, Fleiner talks about the past 25 years in which he travelled all around the world, visiting the offices and facilities of companies he was working for. 'In general, Americans lack a certain sense of the fact that many people outside the USA do not speak English as their native language. Furthermore, every culture has its own way of interacting. Many of my fellow-Americans do not adapt as I slow my speaking down and try to simplify my words so nobody needs to decode them. I want what I say to land and be understood, so everybody can be on the same page and do the job I expect them to do. So I adapt to those I meet.'

Elaborating on his adapting style, Fleiner paints a picture of his experience with the hierarchic working culture at the Korean branch of the company. 'I'm not the kind of CEO who tells you what to do, but the Koreans were used to being directed. I wanted them to start thinking for themselves, but it took quite some time to get that going. My style of leading was authentic. Once they figured that out, they were able to get comfortable and start moving.'

Showtime

After taking the helm at Malvern Panalytical, Fleiner soon discovered that a certain distance had grown between members of the executive management and other employees. To narrow this mystifying gap, he started organising small talks throughout the company, which he insisted should have a personal touch. 'To open up any conversation, especially if we're not very acquainted yet, I find it useful to share something personal: where I come from, how my family's doing, what my passion is – maybe even that I read some great article yesterday. This helps me relate to people and really get in touch. Above all, I always try to converse with energy and enthusiasm.

This gets people in the right mindset and creates an atmosphere in which you can deepen or address the sensitive issues that I call the "pink elephants". These are the issues that everyone knows are in the room but that nobody wants to discuss because they tend to be awkward and uncomfortable.' Fleiner acknowledges that being available all the time with a positive approach can be stressful and tiring. 'As they say in Hollywood, it's always showtime. But if you stay consistent and authentic in your approach and communication, you can move and touch people. That's how I want to function as a business leader.'

Breathe in confidence

Rather than look at what people do right or wrong, Fleiner emphasises that he tries to focus on people's potential. 'I've seen top managers who do not appreciate people asking questions. They're rather straightforward about wrong assumptions and mistakes. I try to let people find answers on their own. If they've come to the wrong solution or conclusion, I let them discover how they got there.'

Not surprisingly, Fleiner knows that compliments do wonders; but his mission goes beyond this managerial trick. 'I want to lead by giving people a certain way to become better. That's not by pointing out their mistakes. I give them the chance to self-evaluate instead. That shows I'm looking out for them. I'm always looking to create or find opportunities where my people can breathe in confidence to make them faster, stronger and better employees for our business.'

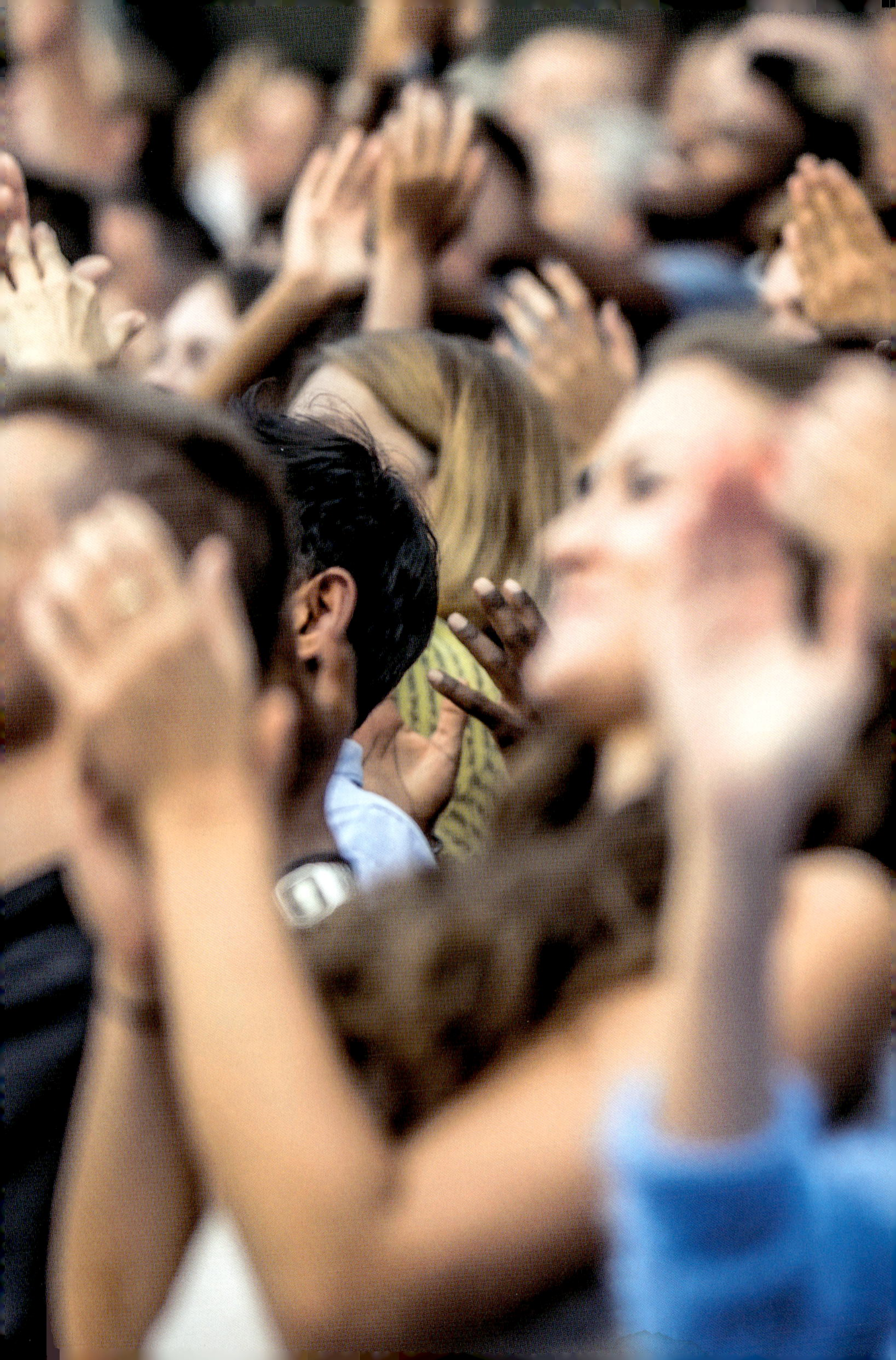

"People will embrace change if they see and understand"

LEADING BY CREATING VALUE

Exposed but not lonely at the top

TALK WITH

THEO SPIERINGS

former CEO of Fonterra
Auckland, New Zealand

Theo Spierings was CEO of Friesland Foods in 2008 when it merged with Campina, creating the third largest dairy cooperation in the world. Another captain took over at that time, and Spierings left the Dutch company. Almost three years later, after several other international assignments, he found himself in New Zealand as he started as the CEO of Fonterra.

Based on the other side of the world, Fonterra did not attract a lot of attention, even though it was (and still is) the largest dairy cooperative globally. 'The company itself has an enormous impact on the country. If it sneezes, the country will catch a cold. The company accounts for about 12 per cent of the national economy. That becomes about 30 per cent if you add the production of our more than ten thousand affiliated farmers.

This has made me a public figure, with kind of the same status as the prime minister or the captain of All Blacks, the national rugby team. Leading this company is like living the life of a famous sportsman, actor or musician.'

Living in a fishbowl
Between 2011 and 2018, Spierings learnt the consequences of this exposed position. Unlike any other CEO, he had to endure constant criticism and the pressure of explaining all big decisions and important moves, not only within the company or to members of the cooperation but also to politics and the general public. 'CEOs can't hide nowadays. There's no doubt about that. They have to be visible, more transparent than ever and empathetic. But for about seven years I lived as the only goldfish in the bowl.
That's more than lonely – I was fully exposed.' Spierings had the benefit of not being the type who wants to show off or live the celebrity life. His wife used her maiden name in Auckland society, and Spierings tried not to stand out. 'You have to lead by setting the right example. Parading on the red carpet or driving big fancy cars will only get you in trouble on social media and lead to criticism or even worse.'

Giving back
His time at the top took its toll. It was one of the main reasons for Spierings to announce his departure as CEO and, at the same time, his initiative for The Purpose Factory. This enterprise, based in his rural home town of Ommen in the Netherlands, is Spiering's way of giving back to society.
'I've been working in cooperatives my entire career. In a cooperative, it's all about creating value for all stakeholders. But CEOs of big companies have to depend on what's decided or happens in board rooms and in politics.
Well, at The Purpose Factory we believe that we can add value by helping other companies contribute to a better world and to get, to be and to stay sustainable. A big advantage is that there's no board, no other shareholders and certainly no prime minister to deal with. So now I'm in charge and can get things done: to get things moving instead of being delayed or obstructed.'

Redistributing created value

With The Purpose Factory, Spierings has committed himself and a team of employees and experts to four of the seventeen Sustainable Development Goals (SDGs) of the UN: no poverty, zero hunger, clean water and sanitation, and climate action. As already said, the mission in cooperatives is to create value and ensure that all stakeholders in the local communities get their share. This is what the Purpose Factory is all about: creating and redistributing value. How do we do that? First, we coach, give guidance and maybe invest in start-ups. Second, we give strategic advice to large companies and help to implement that advice. Third, we support and finance local sustainability initiatives. Since there's no fee for our services unless there's a favourable result, we can decide fast and on our own where to channel our energy and resources. That really excites me.'

MANAGE YOUR COMPANY CULTURE

THE BEHAVIOURAL AGENDA

Lead from your own sweet spot

Winning organizations have strong teams with strong people. So, it starts with the individual team member. Every one of them should bring in the qualities that make them stand out. By owning their part of the challenges ahead, team members are dedicated to deliver. Thus, every team member is a leader in respect of his own sweet spot: the imaginary meeting point between their value and impact, strength and skills and, of course, passion and energy.

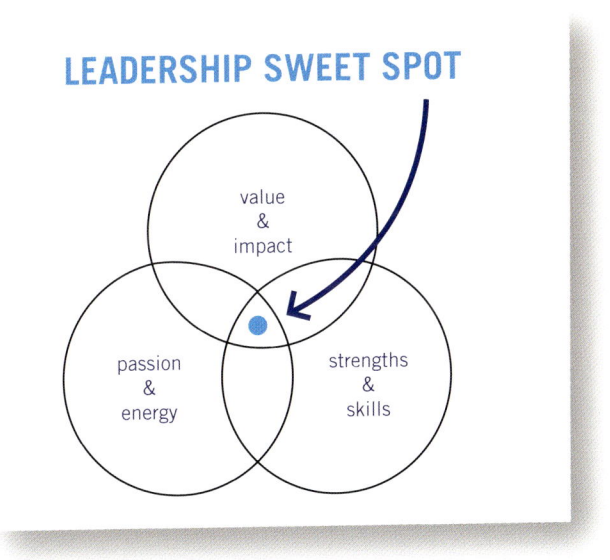

LEADERSHIP SWEET SPOT

- value & impact
- passion & energy
- strengths & skills

Cultural norms define what is encouraged, discouraged, accepted or rejected within a group. When aligned with personal values, drives and needs, culture can unleash tremendous amounts of energy towards a shared purpose and foster an organization's capacity to thrive. When aligned with strategy and leadership, a strong and high trust culture drives positive outcomes.

There are four levers to create a winning culture (Harvard Business Review Jan-Feb 2018)[7]:

1. Articulate the aspiration.
What do we want to achieve? What is the overall purpose and why is this so important? The aspiration needs to be clear, and the plan for how to get there needs to be solid and convincing.

2. Select and develop leaders who align with the target culture.
Who are those people that have the right skills and competencies for the mission we are embarking on? Maybe even more important: do they have the right mindset, values and beliefs to dedicate themselves fully to the job and make it all work?

3. Use organizational conversations about culture to underscore the importance of change.
A good friend of mine always tells me that an organization is a system of conversations. What kinds of encounters can we organise to this end? How can we really connect and talk openly and honestly with each other about working and winning together? We need to be able to discuss the undiscussables in order to outperform.

4. Reinforce the desired change through organizational design.
Real change in an organization comes through people who work with passion and pride on something new and better. It does not come from changing the organigram or a restructuring. However, a new organizational design can, should and must help to reinforce the desired change and help to push it forward.

Think about the Marines. They have a connected community, which comes from the early indoctrination of every member of the corps and the clear communication of their purpose and value system. It is completely clear that they are privileged to be joining an elite community that is committed to improvising, adapting and overcoming in the face of any adversity. The culture is so strong that it glues the community together and engenders a sense of pride that makes them unparalleled. The culture is what each Marine relies on in battle and in preparation. It's an amazing example of a living culture that drives pride and performance. (Dan McGinn, August 2015)[8]

Winning is about getting culture right
Former US Secretary of Defense & retired Marine General James Mattis[9]: 'There are many challenges organizations can overcome, but having a bad culture is not one of them. Culture starts at the top, and a good or a bad leader sets the tone for how the organization does business.'

TOWARDS A WINNING CULTURE

Building a strong culture starts with hiring strong people and working together in strong teams that lead to a strong organization that delivers strong results through a winning culture.

Strong People

In my point of view, strong people are passionate, self-confident and purpose-driven professionals with high energy and a strong orientation towards action. These people preferably also know their stuff and understand the industry. Not only must they be capable and engaged, but they also need to be coached and trained. Above all, you need to lead them in an inspiring way that enhances their self-confidence and self-esteem, so they will speak up, give their opinion and feedback, and engage others. They also need to be able to think big and keep things simple.

Creating a winning mindset starts with self-awareness, observation and self-diagnosis. How is your brain wired? There seems to be a hierarchy in how the human animal in us thinks, feels and behaves:

The way you think will impact how you feel. So what are your winning beliefs?
- What you focus on is what you'll get!
- Together we will win!
- We have done it before, so we will succeed again!
- Have never done this... So I think I can do it!

The way you feel impacts how you behave. What are your winning emotions about?
- Being relaxed, and laughter comes easy
- Feeling pride and commitment
- Showing and feeling passion for what you do

Strong people don't sit and wait

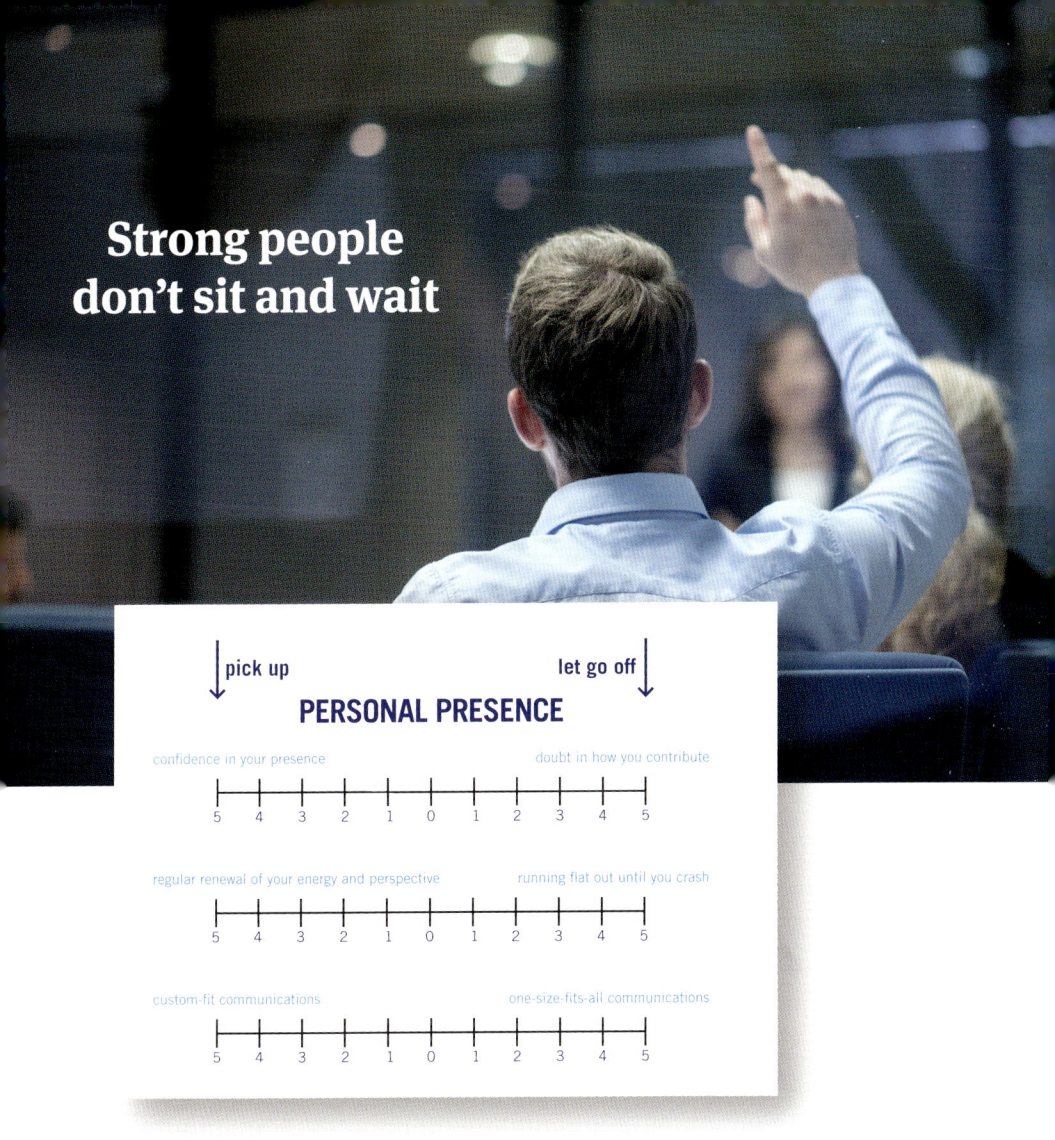

PERSONAL PRESENCE

↓ pick up   let go off ↓

confidence in your presence — doubt in how you contribute
5 4 3 2 1 0 1 2 3 4 5

regular renewal of your energy and perspective — running flat out until you crash
5 4 3 2 1 0 1 2 3 4 5

custom-fit communications — one-size-fits-all communications
5 4 3 2 1 0 1 2 3 4 5

The way you behave will impact your success and achievements. What habits and patterns do you follow?
- Delivering at warp speed
- Having high energy at all times
- Taking massive action once a decision has been made

As a leader, to build a strong personality you need to pick up and let go as well (Scott Eblin, 2006)[10].

Strong team

It's not a natural phenomenon that strong people create strong teams. Teams that have a three-musketeer mentality are defined by mutual trust and have this attitude of 'one for all and all for one'. These teams are like tribes with a code and where nobody is more important than the team.

In his Trombone Player Wanted video, Marcus Buckingham shares two excellent statements: 'High performing teams understand that each member must focus on their strengths. Team members are counting on everybody's full engagement and that the strengths of the one will augment the weakness of the other, enabling the whole to accomplish things that the individual could never do on their own.'

'They also tend to spend quality time getting to know each other, so they can trust each other and rely on each other's judgements. These teams are effective because of their vulnerability, their open communication and their willingness to stimulate productive dialogue within the confines of that team.'

Nobody is more important than the team

Role of managers

Managers play a significant role in creating an environment within which individuals can thrive, discover their talents and be their best selves daily. Great managers help people to identify and leverage their unique strengths. They should not try to reproduce what their best performers do differently, as that often creates greater constraints instead of giving people the freedom to do their best. The trick is to help people put innovative ideas into practice without stifling the personal strengths that give them their edge.

As a leader, to build strong teams you need to pick up and let go as well (Scott Eblin, 2006)[10]:

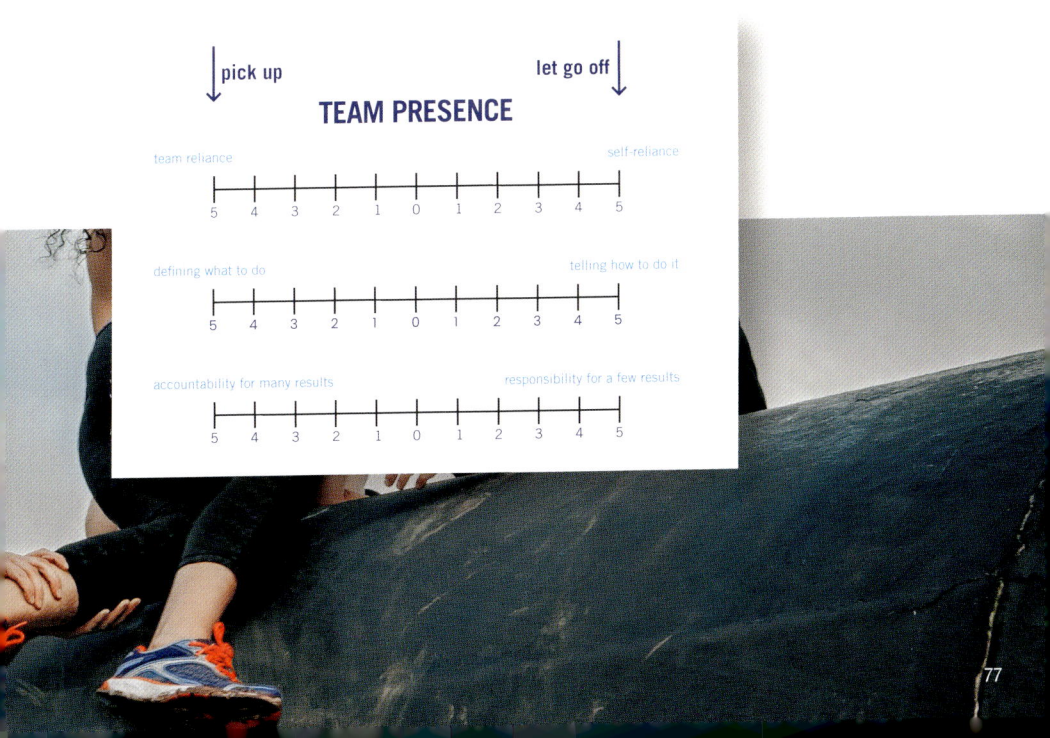

↓ pick up   let go off ↓

TEAM PRESENCE

team reliance   self-reliance
| + + + + + + + + + + |
5 4 3 2 1 0 1 2 3 4 5

defining what to do   telling how to do it
| + + + + + + + + + + |
5 4 3 2 1 0 1 2 3 4 5

accountability for many results   responsibility for a few results
| + + + + + + + + + + |
5 4 3 2 1 0 1 2 3 4 5

STRONG ORGANIZATION

To build these strong teams into a strong organization, you need to get all departments fully aligned. These departments must become aware that collaboration – not working in silos – is key to achieving the company's goals. Instead of complaining about the work of other departments or criticising each other, they should – with the focus on their markets and customers – help out with and complement each other's efforts. Continuous improvement starts with open communication.

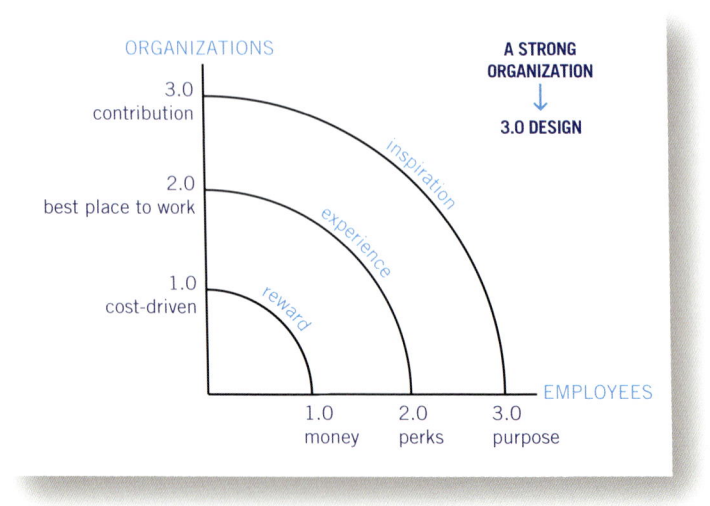

```
ORGANIZATIONS                    A STRONG
   3.0                           ORGANIZATION
contribution                          ↓
                                 3.0 DESIGN
   2.0              inspiration
best place to work
                   experience
   1.0
cost-driven       reward
                                      EMPLOYEES
              1.0       2.0      3.0
             money     perks    purpose
```

It is essential that teams share a clear company vision and mission, and the same values. They have to adopt the same great values and be familiar with the winning strategy and agile structure. Designing a strong organization supports, feeds and nurtures a great, energising and winning company culture:

1.0 Design

Traditionally, many organizations are still cost-driven companies that have contracted money-driven employees who just work to make a living. Reward in money is the driver here both for the individual and the organization.

2.0 Design

Other organizations try to become one of these best places to work to attract employees in a tight labour market. Employees that are on the lookout for a great C&B package with generous company perks work here, and they are well taken care of. They are happy to have this great work experience in a highly tuned and almost pampered work environment. 'I'm having a great time here!' is what drives the workforce.

3.0 Design

In more sustainable organizations, leadership looks at not only the P&L but also to what extent the company contributes to a better world. This is where purpose-driven professionals love to work. Inspiration and passion are key drivers here and become true accelerators.(PI, 2018)[11]

As a leader, to build a strong organization you need to pick up and let go as well (Scott Eblin, 2006)[10]

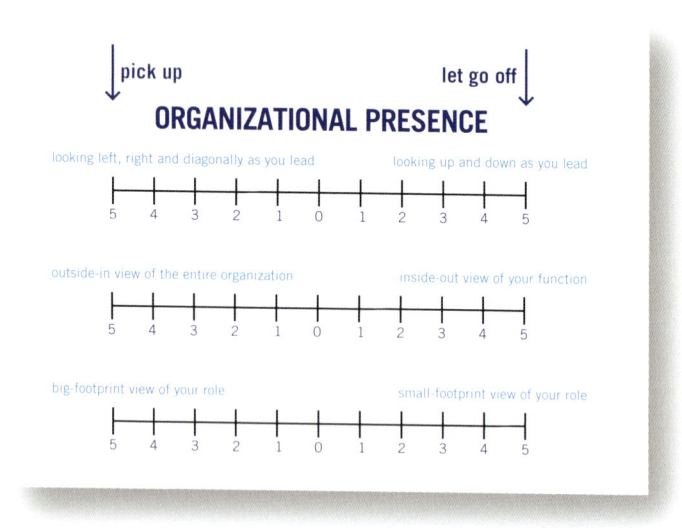

↓ pick up   let go off ↓

ORGANIZATIONAL PRESENCE

looking left, right and diagonally as you lead	looking up and down as you lead
5 4 3 2 1 0	1 2 3 4 5

outside-in view of the entire organization	inside-out view of your function
5 4 3 2 1 0	1 2 3 4 5

big-footprint view of your role	small-footprint view of your role
5 4 3 2 1 0	1 2 3 4 5

Strong results
The result of a strong organization is that customers will recognise that you have a lot to offer: great products, fantastic service, an engaged and purpose-driven workforce, fast delivery with a smile and solid after-sales. They will come back to you to buy more and are willing to pay more for what you bring to the marketplace. They have become raving fans and love you for your great reputation.

Don't try to predict or control complex systems. Instead, focus on making yourself more adaptable and resilient, so you can respond effectively to unexpected events.

In his book "Team of Teams", General Stanley McChrystal[12] presents a new way of thinking and leading that allows organizations to adapt and innovate nimbly in a complex world. To respond fluidly to complex environments, your team must become adaptable and resilient.
This in turn requires that they:
- Learn to expect the unexpected (rather than seek to predict/control the outcomes); and
- Are connected in a way that allows them to rapidly reconfigure themselves to respond to new threats or opportunities.

The agility of small teams is replicated on a large scale through shared consciousness (think & act as a single organism) and empowered execution (make best possible decisions at all levels), both within the organization and externally with partner organizations.

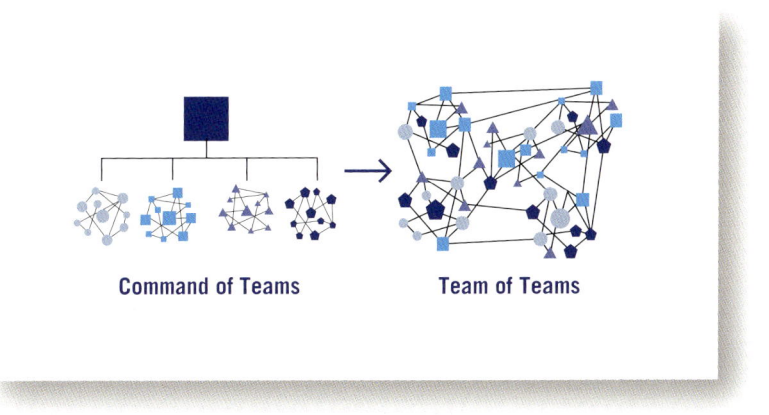

Command of Teams → **Team of Teams**

THE FRAMEWORK FOR WINNING

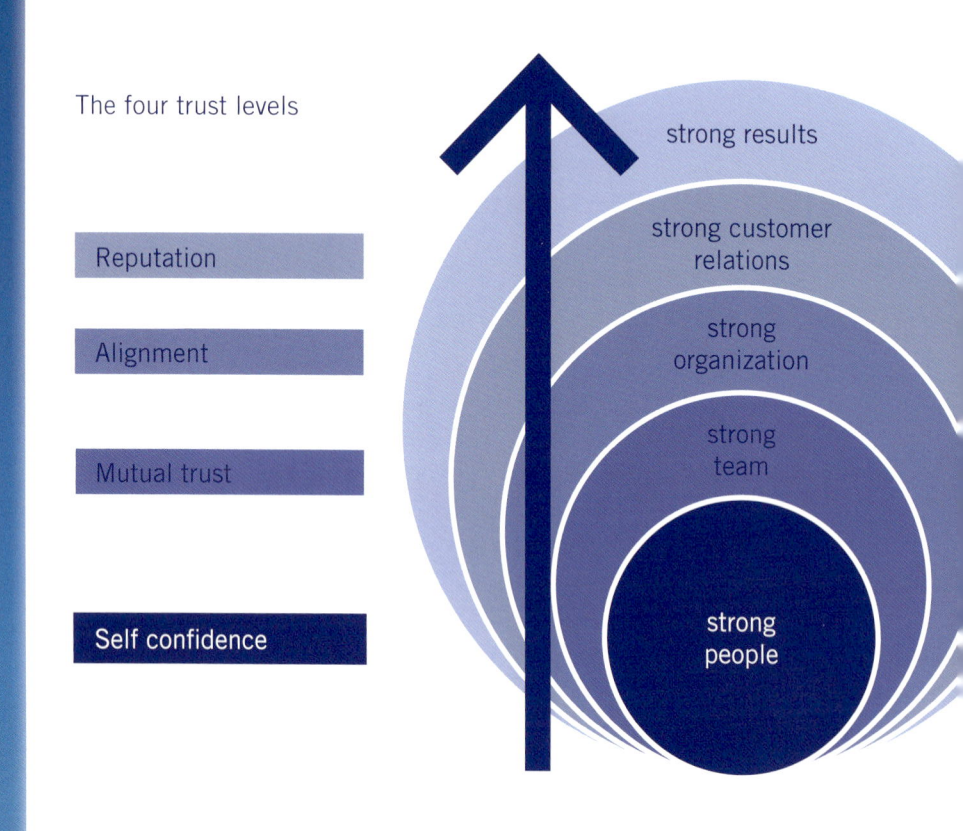

The four trust levels

- Reputation
- Alignment
- Mutual trust
- Self confidence

- strong results
- strong customer relations
- strong organization
- strong team
- strong people

Great & Inspiring Leadership

Turnover, EBIT, etc...

Raving fans

- Clear vision
- Inspiring mission
- Great valeus
- Winning strategy
- Agile structure

Three musketeer attitude & behaviour

Capable and engaged individuals

SEVEN CULTURE KILLERS [13]

1

Arrogance
failing to recognise shifts in the industry/landscape

2

Misalignment
no cultural beacon or behavioural pull for others

3

Lack of clarity
confusion from varying beliefs of what is important

4

Missing employee engagement
a passive or disengaged workforce will cripple efforts to build a strong company culture

5 Failure to embed values
having values that are simply posted on the walls but are not embedded values in everyday aspects

6 Mixed messages
sending different and conflicting messages

7 Talent churn
staff turnover can be a culture killer, or it can be used to save a failing organization

"TRUST IS CRUCIAL IN ANY CIRCUMSTANCE"

Never waste a good crisis

TALK WITH

VALERIA FLEN

CEO of Gloria
in Lima, Peru

Valeria Flen spent most of her first 50 days as the new general manager of Leche Gloria in a hotel room. Because of a strict curfew – enforced by military patrols – the streets of Lima, in Peru, were empty. The country was in total COVID lockdown. 'Well, this crisis helped me to focus on the most critical factors of the business.'

With about 5,000 employees and a well-known brand that is loved throughout the country, Leche Gloria is the dairy industry leader in Peru. However, leading this company and showing it the way forward for the next years would be no walk in the park, not even for Flen with her extensive international experience in the food sector. Over some 30 years, she's held various positions of responsibility in important regional and global companies dedicated to the dairy chain, mainly in Chile and Venezuela. 'The first step was to understand how business worked in Venezuela and to develop a strategic plan that would allow us to survive this unknown crisis in a rather complicated country. The second was to convince the board that there was still hope and to continue betting on the country. The third key topic was to align the team of executives towards the same business purpose, mainly by convincing them that this was vital to feed Venezuelan families.'

Necessary steps

Her outline of which initial steps to take shows Flen's experience with tough projects and situations in previous jobs. Nevertheless, starting this new position as the company's first female CEO during a crisis with huge external influences beyond anyone's control could make one at least a bit nervous. 'Sure, I had to face my fear of the unknown. But I also had to take responsibility for my role. I felt emotionally stable, primarily because I knew Leche Gloria's team needed someone who could stay calm and show a simple and clear path during the crisis. Because of stress, pressure and the need to manage multiple contingencies at once, it would be easy to lose sight of the bigger picture. That's when you lose control.'

Strengthen the spirit

This initial – and unprecedented – period gave Flen a kick-start as she onboarded at Leche Gloria. She felt very welcome and was able to demonstrate her leadership skills from the very beginning. But she knew she had to look beyond that. 'There's a lot of pride and passion for the brand. That had been carefully developed over the years. Hard work and dedication had made Leche Gloria a big organization with a very strong brand. Loyalty and a trustful inner circle created a powerful climate to become the undisputed market leader. But today's marketplace had become more volatile, uncertain and complex. There was also the need to manage contingencies and incidents. That had taken the focus away from designing a vision and strategy for the longer term. So, besides day-to-day management, my goal was to strengthen the company to become a true purpose-driven, future-fit and sustainable organization, led by people with a winning team spirit.'

A straight path and the trust to walk it
Flen says there are several aspects that make a company ready to win in the marketplace and that most of those have to be kept simple. 'But coming up with a solid plan and a straight path to follow is no easy task.'
It all starts with a clear mission perspective on the future and a compelling value system: both must be easy to understand. Once you set your goals, you can start to mobilise and energise people.'

'Having said that, I think that trust is maybe the most important dimension. Take a look at my style of leadership. It's quite democratic. But once we decide on something together, I'm strict about everyone sticking to it. I have to trust that people will take responsibility, own their tasks and deliver. It's during a crisis, like in the first half of 2020, that a company really shows whether these three aspects – trust, own and deliver – are part of its culture.

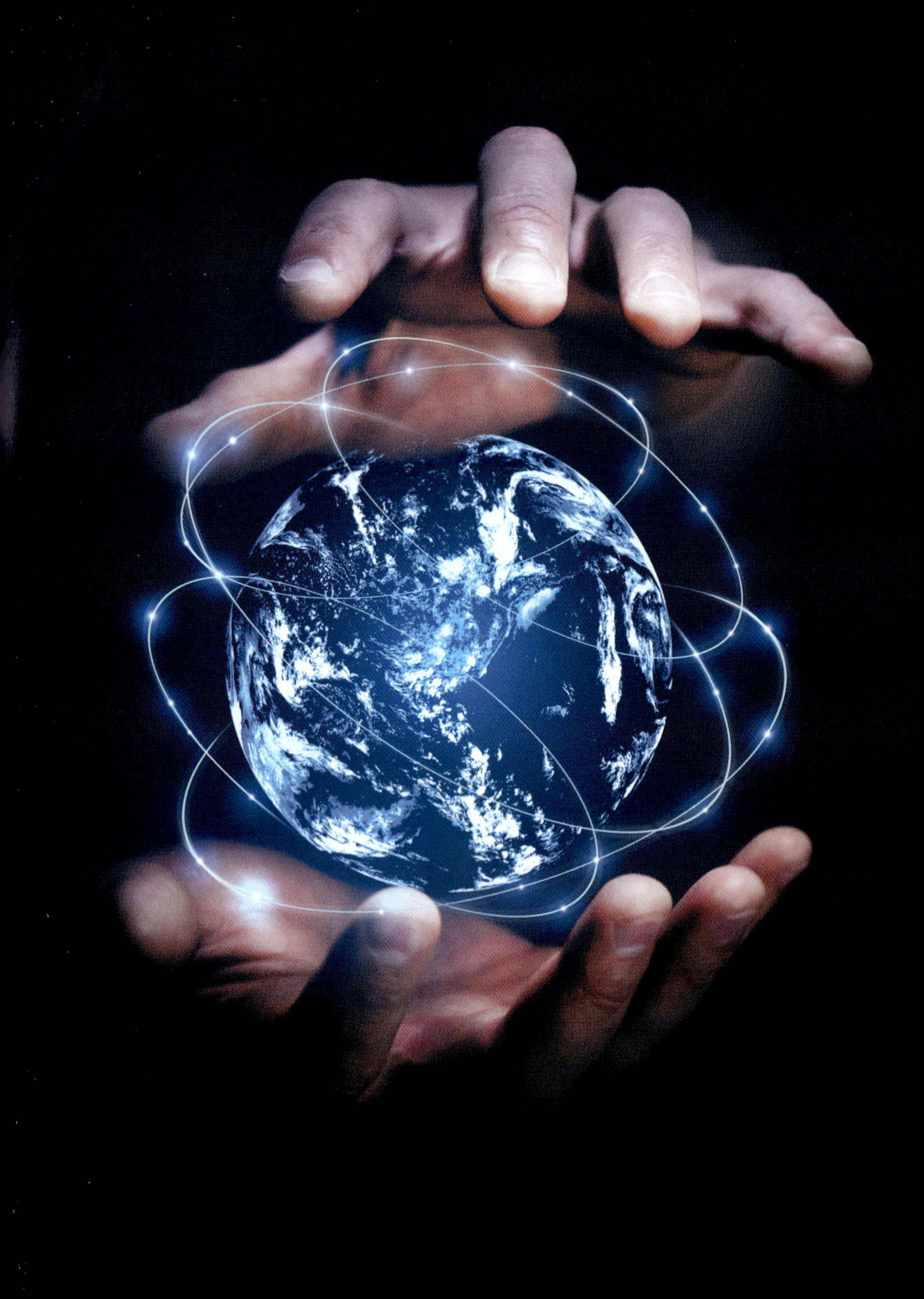

IN THE VUCA WORLD

Getting comfortable with the uncomfortable[14]
Even if you manage to attract strong people, create strong teams and align them into a strong organization, there's still no promise of success. Given today's volatile, uncertain and chaotic business environment, all you've done is made success a possibility. These are some lessons that are perfectly applicable to increase the possibility of being successful:

You are not able to control everything that happens in the world

Push. Work hard, push through and do not give up. This means training yourself to take setbacks and keep on going.

Focus. What needs to be done? Create clarity, have high energy and a laser focus. Get things done.

Power. Be strong, have power and strengthen your body. The body is the temple of your soul. Work out, exercise and make it happen every day. Consistency is key.

Mind. Always be ready for anything. Feed, condition and strengthen your mind every day. Your performance is a reflection of your belief system.

Time. Work quickly, especially if not in a hurry so you have time left when you are in a hurry. Create space and have more bandwidth.

Pressure. Having a capacity for humour, fun and creativity in a stressful environment will define how well you do in times of pressure.

Grow. Understand your limitations and use this to challenge yourself to grow. Deal with criticism and setbacks.

Results. Get more out of the same hours or minutes, cut the crap and work yourself through the clutter of details and get the results you are after.

Team. Nobody is more important than the team. Give more than you expect to receive and add lots of value to others.

Lead. Lead by example and get proximity to amazing people. Put yourself in the game with people who constantly stretch you.

Unleash your potential as a leader

Become a learning leader in this VUCA world by:

1. **Improving your capacity** to reflect and learn to better observe, diagnose and influence.
2. **Really connecting with the outside world:** communicate smarter, reach out to 'others' and use the internet to the max!
3. **Becoming a better visionary:** grow your capacity to envision, strategize and frame the big picture.
4. **Being more agile:** be faster, more flexible and adaptable, creative and action-oriented.

And above all: practise, practise, practise and have someone coach you.

> ### Build the capacity to adapt
> There's no doubt that you need a plan, as explained earlier in the part on the rational agenda. But there's no way that everything will go as you expect. There are far too many uncertain and unexpected aspects, both internal and external, that will influence operations. Even a plan B will not remove the need for flexibility to adapt.

There is this story by General Stanley McChrystal[12] that illustrates this the best:

'When I joined Special Operations as a Green Beret, we were already pretty good at operating as small teams. Inside those teams, you had a chain of command, but you also had a more informal set of linkages. You had constant interaction – the ability to not just hear what people say, but see their actions up close. You get a level of familiarity with teammates, and they get in-depth knowledge of you too. This informal set of interactions is really the magic. The more powerful those informal interactions are, where all it takes is one glance between one person and another, that's how you go from command and control to organic movements.'

'Special Forces spend a lot of time rehearsing missions, but war has become so unpredictable that the value of rehearsal seems to be diminishing. I still believe in rehearsals, but I've learned they have a different value. The longer we rehearsed, the more I realised the value of rehearsal was not in trying to get this perfect choreography. The value of rehearsal was to familiarise everybody with all the things that could happen, what the relationships are and how you communicate.'

LEAVING NO MAN BEHIND

Learning, sharing and adding value

TALK WITH

JORDY KOOL

Entrepreneur & Investor
Noordwijk, the Netherlands

In 1995, two ankle injuries brought an end to Jordy Kool's career in the Marine Corps, an elite group of the Dutch armed forces. It was the beginning of a new and surprising adventure for an entrepreneur whose success seems to come from his thirst for knowledge, incredible eagerness to learn and his firm conviction to add value wherever he can. 'At the same time, I'm always looking for feedback and want people to challenge my ideas. Which is why, even before turning 25, I asked a CEO who I admired to be my mentor. After that, I had the good fortune of being able to ask several very experienced people in top positions for advice and to let me bounce my ideas off them. A couple of them still do that. In turn, I also want to be a mentor for other entrepreneurs.'

Jordy Kool started out in 2009 at Infotheek as its chief commercial officer and became the company's CEO in 2013. He left in 2018 after the company's turnover had grown from 55 million to 800 million euros with him at the helm. In the year 2021, Jordy Kool takes part in 16 businesses via his investment company. He and his team at We Support BV are involved in shaping the vision and strategy of the management board at each of those businesses – not to mention helping with implementation. 'I think I have a good nose for trends and developments in society and am able to channel those into a well-thought-out vision and strategy. But the way that strategy goes is ultimately down to implementation. Great plans have to be well executed, down to the smallest detail, to become reality. That's hard work, and it requires constant focus. As the management, you simply have to be on top of it, so you can take fast action if things go wrong.'

Putting together a team

'I see opportunities and make connections that others don't, and I approach new plans differently. I also see what doesn't work or where improvements could be made in an organization or in a market.'

In his prior management positions, and now as an investor, Kool understands quite well that he needs to put the necessary energy into a business. That starts by deciding who should be in the management team. He's rather pleased to say that the team members need to be good at what he himself doesn't like or what he's not good at; and he emphasises that he doesn't always favour the best candidate. 'I have no use for prima donnas, for people who only want to play in the front line. Even stars like Messi and Ronaldo would be nothing without people who steal and pass the ball or who close the gap.' Kool says his carefully selected team doesn't really come alive until each member is 100% behind the plans and has the will to win. With the famous quote 'culture eats strategy for breakfast' in mind, he takes as much time as needed to explain things and to share his knowledge, motivation and reasons for doing things. 'For proper execution, everyone needs to be united behind the plan and go for it as a team. That's probably more important than fully conforming to my ideas. The only way for us to succeed is to be and feel united. The only time I intervene is if people in the team go different ways. If there's a difference of opinion about really important things, what I say goes.'

Delegating and monitoring

Once the team is aligned and the plans have been hammered out, Kool mainly wants to instil trust and delegate responsibility. 'The latter is inescapable in order to get all the work done. But I'm not naive. You also have to monitor. I see pretty quickly how things are going in a business, such as by walking around the office or having a look at the financials. In addition, we always ensure there's a good information structure where all aspects can be monitored and reported. Based on what I see and analyse, I focus on coaching and supporting the staff. That's how I add value.'

'When people work, they make mistakes. That's okay. The trick is to make sure they start performing better from that point on. That means not only giving them the tools they need but also encouraging and coaching them. And yes, sometimes you have to show them how: set a good example.'

Band of brothers

Kool's dedication to the team, and achieving the right mindset, goes far. 'My goal is a band of brothers where people rally each other, are there for each other when needed and want to make everyone better. I see that as my task, and that's also the task of the management under my direction. Everyone needs to be focused on improving the performance of their co-workers and immediate colleagues in addition to their own individual performance, of course.'

Kool doesn't feel that people should be ditched if they start lagging behind and don't produce the necessary quality of work. 'If people aren't performing as well or don't feel comfortable in their role, we help them reconnect, no matter how. The principle of "we leave no man behind" is really deeply rooted in me. Once you're part of the team, we make sure you're able to stay part of it.' On the other hand, Kool demands maximum loyalty. 'If you're not playing along with the team and won't stick to the game plan, you'll eventually have to answer to me. When that time comes, I'll try to be gentle, but I'll certainly make my point. I won't mince words. Some things just have to be said, even if some people have a hard time with that. Sometimes I have to accept that's going to dent the relationship. That's usually temporary, luckily.'

How to build a team
Building a team that performs well starts with putting together the right people and creating a good structure. 'After that, I require the necessary discipline. I'm always clear about the rules of engagement: what do I expect from you, for the business and for the team? Besides that, it just takes a lot of hard work, and it needs to be enjoyable too. People also need to be properly rewarded. And above all, you need to spend a lot of time on communication. What are we doing? What do we want to achieve?
And how are we going to accomplish that together? These are the questions that I constantly ask – and to which I myself provide the answer.'

Learning more all the time

Everyone has their own definition of wealth. Jordy Kool has even more than one. Aside from being quite comfortable financially, his goal is always to acquire more knowledge, experiences, activities and sometimes even more businesses. 'I always want to keep learning, developing myself and adding value somewhere.'

His career – where he's never dodged a challenge – is proof of that. It was after his much-too-short career as a marine that he began studying for a degree, which took him from International Business to an MBA, from programmes for executives (Harvard) to master classes in mergers and acquisitions, restructuring and corporate governance. The list is long. This is what enabled him to realise and solidify his own personal development in the past twenty years: from account director and young entrepreneur to investor and board member.

While he does sometimes stand in as a part-time CEO at one of the 16 businesses in which he's invested, Kool's aim since 2018 has been to take on non-executive positions, such as currently at a hospital and several NGOs, like IT4Kids. 'Something different is expected from me in those positions, which I find very exciting. There's a difference between sitting on a supervisory board and being the boss of your own company, but I've found it easy to switch back and forth and own the position.

Giving back

Kool is also involved in several projects and active in other sectors and countries that are relatively new to him, such as the USA and North Africa. 'There's always something new to learn, from language to history, from culture to business. That keeps me learning, developing myself and adding value, which means I'm often able to give back to others, to society.'

BITS AND BYTES ON PERSONAL LEADERSHIP

Simple stuff brings energy

High energy is key for success in business and winning in the marketplace. This goes for businesses as well as individuals. When on high energy, your quality of thinking goes up. You are more creative, more productive and smarter. The key here is also not to complicate life; keep things as simple as possible. Leadership is about creating simplicity. Simple ideas, concepts and strategies are easier to understand.

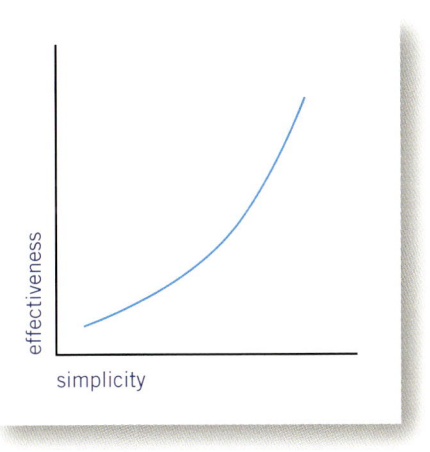

effectiveness vs simplicity

Simplicity versus complexity

Management has to do with dealing with and handling complexity. As complexity is the enemy of execution, simplicity is your biggest friend here.

There are a few guidelines to remember:

- When the going gets tough, carve out time, think things over and brainstorm next steps
- Good and simple plans are never easy to make – persist!
- It takes a lot to come up with a solid plan with full clarity and a straight direction
- Explain your simple plan with a clear story: be concise, clear and talk straight
- If it's stupid but it works, it's not stupid

Influencing others starts with influencing number one

Being successful as a leader begins with a great state of body and mind. Make sure that you focus on your vitality and personal power by:

- Exercising and training the body
- Sleeping well and enough
- Feeding the body with great nutrition
- Staying mentally balanced
- Feeling relaxed
- Having fun with others
- Having and showing passion as a professional

Are you emotionally fit?

Tony Robbins[15] tells us that emotional fitness or a state of readiness is key. Having a capacity for humour, curiosity, compassion and creativity in a stressful environment will grow your flexibility and emotional strength. How well do you do in times of chaos? What is your capacity to bring that sense of certainty, creativity, vision and direction to times of uncertainty?

Action cures fear

The antidote to fear is action. Success never comes to those that just sit and wait. True leaders understand their own capabilities and limitations and use this insight to consistently challenge themselves to grow. How do you react to criticism and setbacks?

Professional development is a key component of leadership, whether it means working on your communication skills, technical acumen or trying something new altogether.

Communicate with Impact

The quality of your leadership depends on how you deliver your talk, speech or presentation. What you say must be consistent with how you say it. The words themselves will not work this magic: you need to deliver with conviction, passion and impact. Most leaders underestimate this force, possibly making it one of the most underutilised tools in business: powerful, empathic and clear communications with high impact on all stakeholders.

So how can you communicate with more impact?
1. Create rapport, find common ground and establish connection
2. Be aware of both your agenda and theirs
3. Observe and diagnose others and figure out what drives them
4. Engage in conversation instead of being Captain Obvious who delivers a boring presentation
5. Educate and empower your audience
6. Create impact by:
    – being an authority (know your stuff)
    – being likeable (kindness is wisdom)
    – being unique (do cool stuff!)

THREE PERSONAL LEADERSHIP QUALITIES THAT ARE ESSENTIAL TO WIN

INFLUENCE
'Engaging, Educating & Empowering others'

Leaders are masters of influence. They know how to propel themselves and motivate & inspire others. High energy is key!

They listen first. It values others.

They use Storytelling to make it relevant to others.

Sharing ideas, asking for help and offering support is what they do.

Passionate professionals know their stuff, want to create impact and win over others. And remember, it's always showtime!

RECOURCEFULNESS
'Getting things done'

Resourcefulness is creating something out of nothing. Get things done.

Lack of recources like time, money and people are never the problem. The real problem is lack of creativity & resourcefulness.

Thinking & Doing are equally important.

DECISIVENESS
'Better decisions sooner'

Your power as a leader comes from your ability to be decisive and having the guts to make tough desicions. In moments of decision your destiny is shaped.

Many people waste time over making the right decision; as a leader you must be willing to draw a line in the sand and make a decision.

When you do, you can positively shape your life and lives of people around you.

Decisiveness is not about waiting, but about speed and taking initiative.

CHECKLIST

Bill Murphy (Inc.com, 2016)[16] has this quick & simple frame to stay focused and challenges us as leaders to discuss these themes & questions every day with our people and then observe what happens:

- [ ] **This is the situation.**
People want to know what's going on. Odds are, they'll find out anyway, or worse, fill in the gaps with conjecture. When you keep important things excessively close, you sap morale, rob yourself of your team's insights, and make people feel undervalued.

- [ ] **Here is the plan.**
A leader is supposed to lead. People will offer great suggestions, especially if you're saying and doing everything else on this list, but you need to be able to make decisions and stand behind them. Your team needs to know where you're trying to take them, and how.

- [ ] **What do you need?**
This is crucial for two reasons. First, people need to know that you care about them on personal and professional levels, and that you want them to succeed. Second, if you've put together a great plan, you need to leverage every person's abilities to the maximum extent possible.

- [ ] **Tell me more.**
Let people know you're more interested in finding good answers than hearing yourself speak. Give others implicit permission to share their opinions--or heck, invite them explicitly, if you have to. Staying quiet is an invitation for others to offer ideas and insights.

☐ **I trust you.**
If you can't trust the people on your team, then they shouldn't be on your team. You need to trust their integrity, their judgment, their confidence and their passion-and you need to ensure that they understand how much you depend on them.

☐ **You can count on me.**
If your team can't trust you, they shouldn't do you the great honour of letting you lead them. So tell them you've got their back, and then work like hell to fulfil the promises you make.

TIP! Write a manifesto

A Personal Leadership Manifesto creates clarity & direction on how you want to lead and win. Key if you want success & strong results. Write one!

- To lead yourself
- To lead your family
- To lead your team
- To lead your organization
- To lead your clients
- To lead society

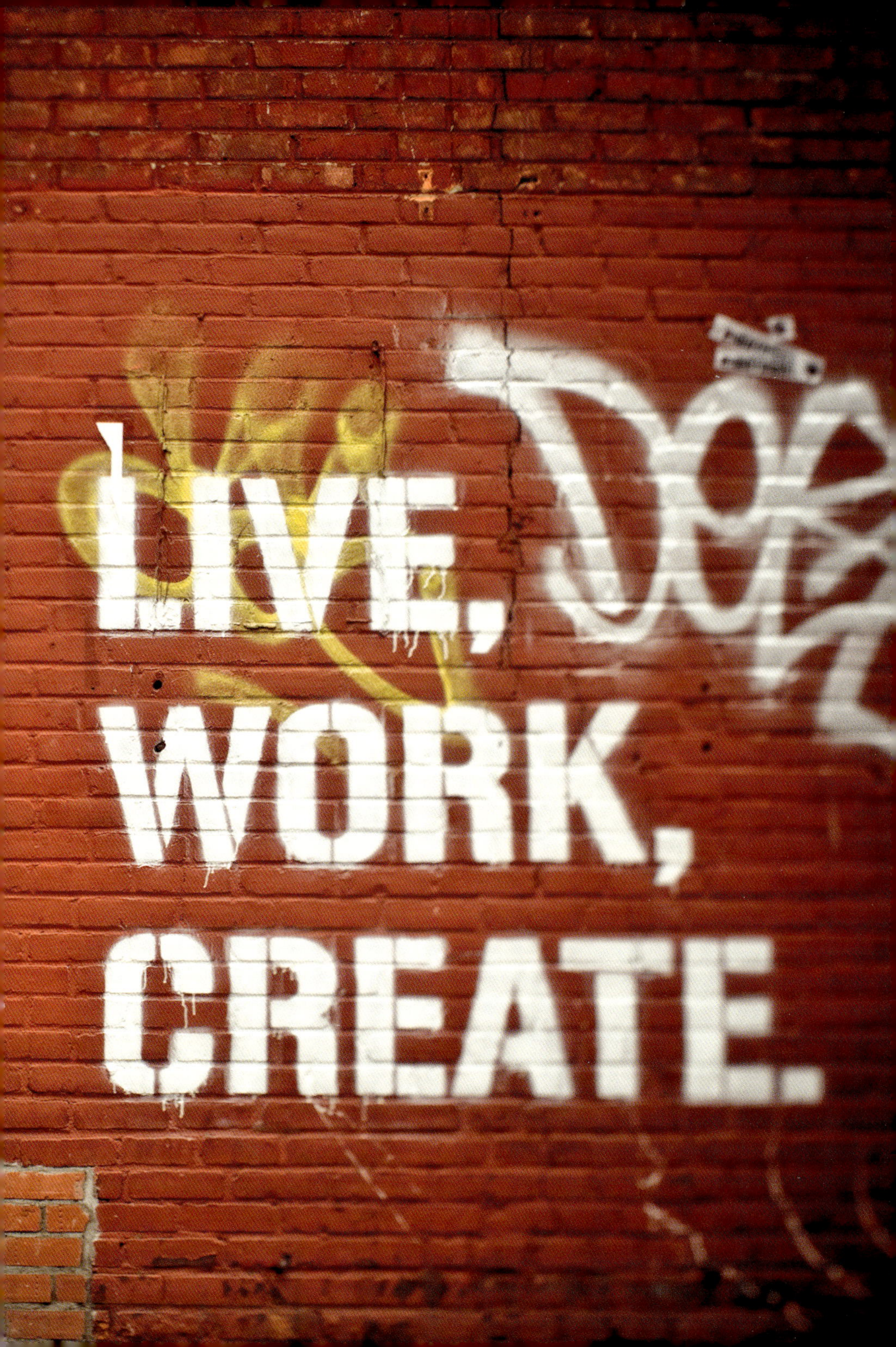
LIVE,
WORK,
CREATE.

CHANGING MAKES US HAPPY

A winning team is like a jazz band

TALK WITH

MARTIN BOEHM

Former Dean of IE Business School, currently Rector EBS University Madrid, Spain

'Today we're facing more and bigger challenges than ever before', says Martin Boehm, former Dean of IE Business School in Madrid. As the speed of societal change increases – with even more complex and diverse challenges in its wake – he's clear about where the real leadership must come from in the near future. 'I don't think that these challenges can be met by governments; they are only here to guide. The real solutions must come from individuals who stand up and companies that lead. Take Tesla, for example. I don't know whether their real mission is to create a more sustainable world, but they're doing a good job, and that seems to be profitable. In a way, they're banking on the growing needs and concerns in the world.'

Style of leadership
As he sketches out the world's problems, like climate change and societal injustice, he emphasises that these problems must be dealt or coped with in unison. 'We teach students to work in teams and collaborate in order to get the best results. One of the principles is that you have to build a team which can be effective. That's not a team where all players excel at the same thing. You need something more like a jazz ensemble, with everyone playing on different instruments and, one by one, taking the lead with a solo, with everyone adapting and staying in sync the whole time.' Boehm says that next to cognitive skills, it's important for students to develop other capabilities, skills and mentalities. Besides being a team player, they also need critical thinking, the ability to solve complex problems and communication skills.

New generations and self-confidence
Boehm emphasises the importance of self-confidence, which he feels is lacking in younger generations. 'More than ever, parents nowadays do almost everything for their kids, and they do that out of love. While this protective environment might seem great, I see it as counterproductive. These kids don't develop the confidence of being on their own, being an independent person. Or they grow up taking things for granted and thinking they rule the world. But look around you: the future has become more precarious and uncertain for new professionals. Therefore, I'd like my kids to be self-confident, self-supporting and independent, so they can adapt and be self-reliant.'

Staying relevant
Self-reliance is all the more important because of the need to adapt to the rapid changes in society and business, says Boehm. In mind of his school's motto of reinventing higher education, the dean says that professionals have to reinvent themselves every five to ten years nowadays.
'We're training our students for jobs that don't exist yet. It's a safe bet that eighty per cent of all jobs that we'll be seeing in three years don't exist today. Change is all around us, and it's only going faster.'

No more straight line to retirement
'When I was young, the career path seemed pretty clear. After four to six years of study you'd get a job or, rather, a profession.
From there on, it would be a straight line (maybe with some promotions or different employers) to retirement, all the while staying in the same profession. Nowadays, this has become uncertain.
So besides a good general education, you need to develop a different set of skills, like empathy, creativity, self-awareness, communication and digital savviness.'

So our school is committed not only to educating students but also to engaging with them and empowering them. This is how we give them the tools to adapt and make the necessary changes in their careers and to stay relevant.'

'Facing the unknown can make a person unsure, but the bottom line is that it's just how you look at it. So why not see the unknown as an exciting new possibility? If you appreciate the challenge and the opportunities, change can even make you happy. You'll have to stay positive and optimistic and see setbacks as a learning experience, but if you're in sync with yourself you'll be able to change your professional life more frequently. That's not gambling with your career: it's just changing your objectives.'

Ecosystem
When Martin Boehm talks about the way academia could work together, and with corporations and NGOs, he speaks of an ecosystem. 'Step by step, we're building a network of business schools where we can collaborate on research and create a better learning experience. I believe this will enrich us, as we develop a framework for how to stay competitive along the way.'

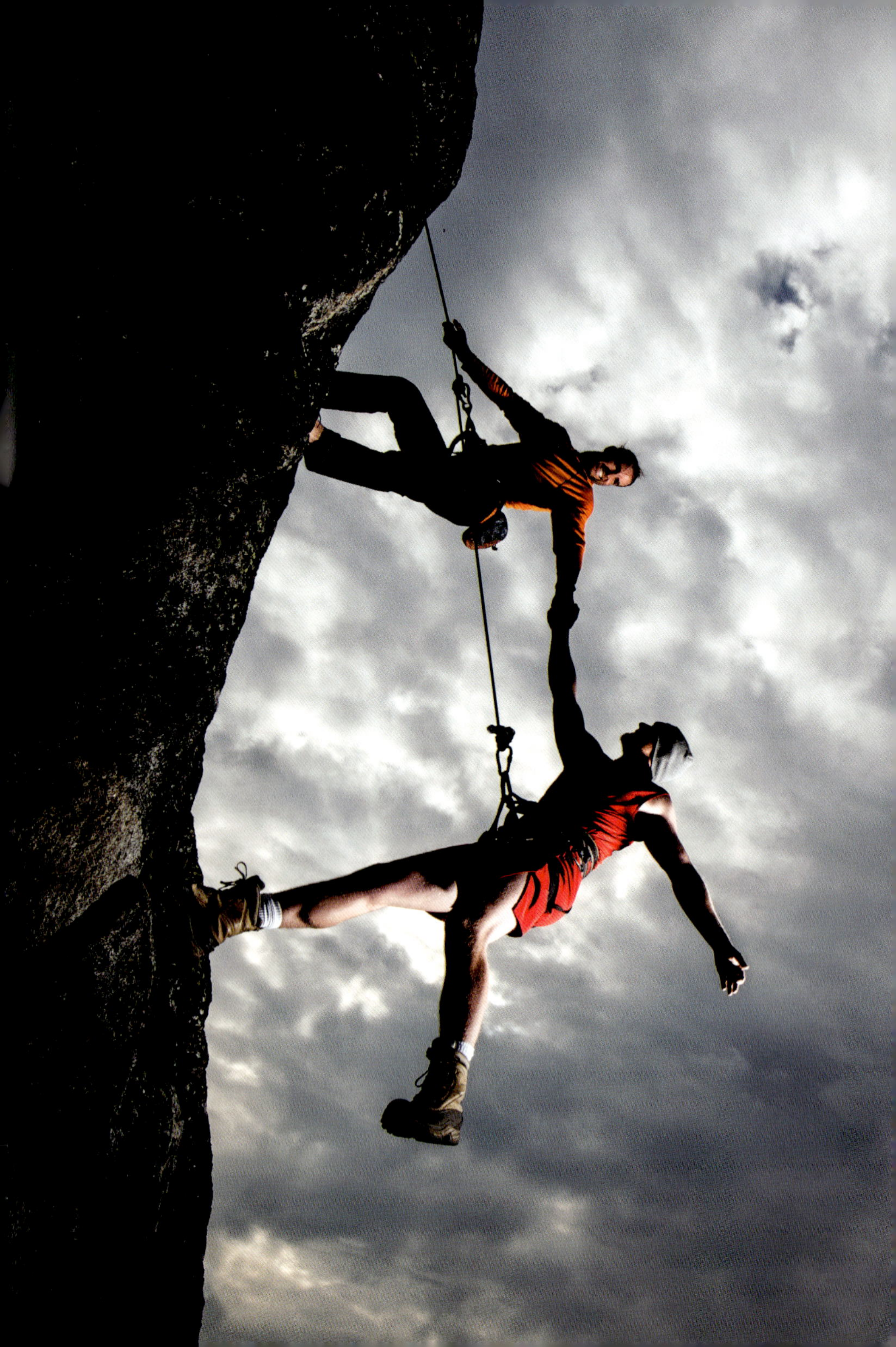

EPILOGUE

On Winning…
Creating a winning company culture in itself is not a complicated thing to do. The basics are quite simple and pretty clear. However, implementing a winning culture is never easy as it requires consistency, energy and discipline. It takes a little time as well.

But let me ask you first if you are a winner? How well do you live? Are you winning? Is your family winning? Are your team and company winning? You cannot take anything for granted in life. There is no free lunch or an easy formula for winning. Keeping the snakes in the zoo happy and waiting for success to come is not a winning strategy. Nor is hoping or praying.

Winning is about stretching yourself to get the most out of life. Sometimes that is not easy. It depends on the season as well. When life in the summer is sunny, easy and generous, it might not be so hard to win. In the harsh winter season, however, you need to be a warrior to fight your way forward in business. The trick to winning is to be able to do well in any season and any environment.

Winning is first about leading yourself:
- Combine logic (the rational agenda) and magic (the emotional agenda)
- Slow down first to do this; you can speed up to go fast after that
- Make sure you are at your best when you deliver
- Be the 'relaxed version' of you when you climb the stage

Having high energy all the time is what often drives personal success.
I run a management consultancy as a business. As a business owner, I need high energy in order to win and expand. Dealing with all kinds of business challenges and finding new horizons feeds and conditions the mind.
It creates emotional fitness: a critical factor for winning in life and business.

Once you're in control of yourself, make sure you get three more things in place for winning:

1. SOLID STRATEGY
a clear vision and a compelling future that engages everyone

2. SOUND STORY
a clear, solid and credible narrative that people can believe in

3. STRONG STATE
a high-energy climate where people love to work

Here's to winning on your journey!

BACKGROUND AND CREDENTIALS

Erik Hiep is an associate professor at IE Business School in Madrid and founded, together with his partner Liesbeth Pruijs, the management consultancy firm The Next Level in 2002. He has extensive consulting experience with international management teams and boards and has worked for a wide variety of clients in more than 30 countries in Europe, the Middle East, Africa, Asia and the Americas.

Erik learned about winning cultures early in his army career as an infantry officer as well as during his time as an executive with Randstad Staffing services.

Creating winning cultures has always been his company's sweet spot and Erik has been teaching about 'winning' for more than 15 years now at IE Business School. In 2018, Erik interviewed former UK Prime Minister David Cameron live on stage before a 2000+ audience at the Breaking Barriers Summit.

Erik holds an MBA from the University of Glasgow and graduated with distinction from the Royal Military Academy in the Netherlands (Infantry and Faculty of Social Sciences and Psychology).

Change starts with reaching out to your people

INDEX OF LITERATURE

1. Pettigrew, AM, Woodman, RW, & Cameron, KS, (2001), Studying Organizational Change and Development August 2001

2. Aristotle, Ars Rethorica Oxford March 1963

3. https://www.ie.edu/building-resilience/knowledge/everything-around-diverts-complexity-go-back-basics/

4. Hersey, P. and Blanchard, K. H. Management of Organizational Behavior 1977

5. https://zengerfolkman.com/white-papers

6. Ten Fatal Flaws That Derail Leaders. By Jack Zenger & Joseph Folkman, HBR Magazine June 2009

7. Harvard Business Review Jan-Feb 2018 'The Leaders guide to Corporate Culture'

8. What companies can learn from military teams Dan McGinn August 2015

9. Leadership lessons from General James Mattis, Business Insider July 2014

10. The Next Level, Scott Eblin, May 2006

11. Prof.Dr. Lidewey van der Sluis, Presidents Institute Seminar 2018

12. Team of Teams by General Stanley McChrystal, 2015 (visuals from ReadinGraphics)

13. www.aon.com/human-capital-consulting/thought-leadership/

14. https://www.ie.edu/insights/infographics/ten-lessons-of-leadership-getting-comfortable-with-the-uncomfortable/

15. 'I am not your guru' by Tony Robbins on Netflix July 2016

16. Bill Murphy in Inc.com, 2016

NOTES

NOTES

NOTES

NOTES

NOTES